Cambridge Elements

Elements in the Philosophy of Physics
edited by
James Owen Weatherall
University of California, Irvine

FOUNDATIONS OF GENERAL RELATIVITY

Samuel C. Fletcher
University of Minnesota, Twin Cities

CAMBRIDGE
UNIVERSITY PRESS

Shaftesbury Road, Cambridge CB2 8EA, United Kingdom

One Liberty Plaza, 20th Floor, New York, NY 10006, USA

477 Williamstown Road, Port Melbourne, VIC 3207, Australia

314–321, 3rd Floor, Plot 3, Splendor Forum, Jasola District Centre,
New Delhi – 110025, India

103 Penang Road, #05–06/07, Visioncrest Commercial, Singapore 238467

Cambridge University Press is part of Cambridge University Press & Assessment,
a department of the University of Cambridge.

We share the University's mission to contribute to society through the pursuit of
education, learning and research at the highest international levels of excellence.

www.cambridge.org
Information on this title: www.cambridge.org/9781009517782

DOI: 10.1017/9781108954082

First published 2024

A catalogue record for this publication is available from the British Library.

ISBN 978-1-009-51778-2 Hardback
ISBN 978-1-108-94928-6 Paperback
ISSN 2632-413X (online)
ISSN 2632-4121 (print)

Foundations of General Relativity

Elements in the Philosophy of Physics

DOI: 10.1017/9781108954082
First published online: November 2024

Samuel C. Fletcher
University of Minnesota, Twin Cities

Author for correspondence: Samuel C. Fletcher, scfletch@umn.edu

Abstract: This Element provides a somewhat comprehensive interpretation of general relativity, a description of what reality would be like if the theory were true. This concerns (i) what possibilities it represents, (ii) the internal structure of those possibilities and their interrelations, and, to some extent, (iii) how those possibilities differ from what's come before. By providing an interpretive foil that one can amplify or amend, it aspires to shape the research agenda in the foundations of general relativity for established philosophers of physics, graduate students searching for work in these topics, and other interested academics. This title is also available as Open Access on Cambridge Core.

Keywords: interpretation of general relativity, ontology of spacetime, energy in general relativity, relativistic causality, time in general relativity

ISBNs: 9781009517782 (HB), 9781108949286 (PB), 9781108954082 (OC)
ISSNs: 2632-413X (online), 2632-4121 (print)

Contents

1 Interpreting Relativistic Spacetimes

In 1919, four years after Albert Einstein completed his formulation of the general theory of relativity, the English astronomer Arthur Eddington organized two expeditions to test its prediction of the deflection of light around massive objects. Their observations of starlight around the Sun during a solar eclipse vindicated Einstein's theory and brought it immediate worldwide attention, including its apparently revolutionary implications for the nature of time, space, and scientific methodology (Ryckman 2005).[1] Having passed all subsequent tests yet made of it, that theory – now commonly known by the moniker "general relativity" (GR) – is currently our best theory of space, time, gravitation, and the cosmos. It is thus still an essential source from which we paint the scientific image of the world.

Painting that image is the business of interpreting GR: metaphysically, depicting what the world, or parts of it, could be like if the theory were true; semantically, giving the truth conditions of the theory's commitments. A *partial* interpretation, then, is an unfinished canvas, depicting *some* aspects of what could be or giving *some* truth conditions. For instance, it may describe the fundamental ontology and properties without advancing any thesis about the metaphysics of properties. What Curiel (2009, 46) calls a "concrete" interpretation is at least a partial interpretation, for it "expresses the empirical knowledge the framework contains – for example, the fixation of a Tarskian family of models, or, less formally, the contents of a good, comprehensive textbook" like Synge (1960), Hawking and Ellis (1973), Misner et al. (1973), Wald (1984), or Malament (2007, 2012).[2] A "concrete" interpretation thus depicts, using interpretive principles, at least what could be empirically.

An example of such a "concrete" interpretation starts with the "pure" gravitational models that abstract away from matter. These are the smooth, four-dimensional Lorentzian manifolds (M, g). They represent ways that a universe or a portion of a universe could be. Those that represent possible universes are sometimes termed *cosmological*. The points of the manifold M represent atomic events, which have no extension or duration, such as an idealized finger snap that gets shorter and smaller without limit; the smooth structure of the points represents how these events are connected together in a four-dimensional continuum modeled locally on $\mathbb{R}^4$. This means that each

---

[1] See Crelinsten (2006) and Kennefick (2019) for details about the expeditions and later controversies about their results.

[2] In what follows, I assume familiarity with the differential geometry these textbooks use in formulating GR. For lack of space and in light of the often voluminous physics literature, I also often cite only recent philosophical reviews of topics in which many further references can be found.

of the three spatial dimensions and the one temporal dimension are modeled (again, locally) on $\mathbb{R}$. Because of this interpretation in terms of events, there are a few topological restrictions on M:[3]

1. M is *Hausdorff*. This ensures any two distinct atomic events can be separated as being parts of disjoint, extended, composite events.
2. M is *path-connected*. A path or curve in M is a continuous function $\gamma: I \to M$, with $I \subseteq \mathbb{R}$ a connected interval, so being path-connected ensures that any two points lie on a common path. This ensures that all events are a part of the same connected continuum.
3. M is *second countable*. This ensures that the collection of events is not so large that a smooth derivative operator (discussed later in this section) or metric cannot be defined on it (Geroch 1971, Marathe 1972). For example, it precludes collections of events based on the long line (Steen & Seebach 1978, 71).

Ultimately, the interpretation of M in terms of events and the concomitant restrictions on the structure of M derive from the interpretation of the spacetime metric g. It represents the durations, lengths, and other derived and related quantities of certain classes of events. Showing how requires some preliminary elaboration. The metric mathematically is a smooth pseudo-Riemannian metric tensor field, meaning that it smoothly assigns a symmetric bilinear form g_{ab} to the tangent space T_pM of each point $p \in M$. (Here, and in what follows, I have the occasion to use the abstract index notation, on which see, e.g., Wald [1984] or Malament [2012].) That the metric has a Lorentzian signature means that one of its four eigenvalues (in any orthogonal basis) is of the opposite sign as the other three. Thus, in each tangent space T_pM, there is a double cone, emanating from the origin, of vectors v^a satisfying $g_{ab}v^av^b = 0$. Appropriately, the vectors in these cones are called *null* or sometimes *lightlike*; those in the interior are called *timelike* and those in the exterior are called *spacelike*. The justification for these labels comes from a certain mathematical fact about curves and a set of representational principles. The mathematical fact is that tangent vectors at p represent directions in the manifold in which a C^1 curve $\gamma : I \to M$ passing through p can point. Such curves can then be classified as null (lightlike), timelike, or spacelike when all their tangent vectors have these respective labels. If v^a is the tangent vector field to any such curve γ, then the *magnitude* of the curve, $|\gamma|$, is defined as $\int_I |g_{ab}v^av^b|^{1/2}ds$, where the integrand is called the magnitude of the vector v^a. Note that $|\gamma|$ is invariant under reparameterization,

---

3 See Geroch and Horowitz (1979) for an extended, accessible discussion.

so curves with the same image have the same magnitude. The first pair of representational principles pertain to certain of these curves:

Duration γ is timelike if and only if $|\gamma|$ represents the *duration* of the events in $\gamma[I]$. (This principle is sometimes called the *clock hypothesis* for reasons to which I turn in Section 2.2, where I also discuss the justification of this and other representational principles.)

Length γ is spacelike if and only if $|\gamma|$ represents the *length* of the events in $\gamma[I]$.[4]

That timelike curves have duration while spacelike curves have length in part justifies the names "timelike" and "spacelike" for their respective sets of tangent vectors. For example, a timelike curve might represent a process or a person's history, and the curve's magnitude the duration of that process or history. These principles entail that every atomic event has zero duration and length, as well as the other features I attributed to them earlier in this section.

In addition to representing durations and lengths, the metric provides a criterion of change for the (signed) magnitude of a vector field u^a along a curve γ: u^a is constant in (signed) magnitude with respect to g_{ab} just in case the scalar field $g_{ab}u^a u^b$ is constant on γ. A (covariant) derivative operator (or "affine connection") ∇_a provides another criterion of change. (As alluded to before, these operators exist globally if and only if M is second countable.) If, as before, v^a is the tangent vector field to γ, then $v^b \nabla_b u^a$ is the directional derivative of u^a along γ, which vanishes just in case u^a is constant with respect to ∇_a on γ. (Both notions of constancy can be generalized to any tensor field on M.) In general, there will be infinitely many derivative operators on M, but the Levi-Civita derivative operator is the unique, torsion-free one *compatible* with the metric, in the sense that a vector field along a curve is constant with respect to the derivative operator only if it is constant in magnitude with respect to the metric. (Compatibility is equivalent with the computationally useful equation $\nabla_a g_{bc} = \mathbf{0}$.) In this sense, the Levi-Civita derivative operator *extends* the notion of change provided by the metric.

A derivative operator determines a Riemann curvature tensor field $R^a{}_{bcd}$, which encodes how the operators ∇_c and ∇_d fail to commute, as represented by the path-dependence of parallel transport of vectors. $R^a{}_{bcd}$ in turn determines the Ricci tensor field $R_{ab} = R^c{}_{abc}$ and, with the metric, the scalar curvature field $R = R_{ab}g^{ab}$. The Einstein field equation (EFE) correlates these curvatures – hence the structure of durations and lengths – with the energy–momentum

---

[4] One can add principles supplemental to **Length** for representing areas, volume, and angles in the obvious way, the former two using the volume measure induced on metric submanifolds, and the latter using the usual cosine formula.

tensor, T_{ab}, which describes the distribution of energy and momentum across spacetime:

$$R_{ab} - \frac{1}{2}Rg_{ab} - \Lambda g_{ab} = \frac{8\pi G}{c^4}T_{ab}, \tag{1}$$

where Λ is the cosmological constant, G is Newton's gravitational constant, and c is the speed of light in vacuum. Eq. (1) shows that the metric, through curvature, determines the distribution of energy and momentum. The trace of Eq. (1) is $(8\pi G/c^4)T = -R - 4\Lambda$, which, when combined with that equation, yields its "trace-reversed" form,

$$R_{ab} = \frac{8\pi G}{c^4}\left(T_{ab} - \frac{1}{2}Tg_{ab}\right) - \Lambda g_{ab}, \tag{2}$$

where $T = T_{ab}g^{ab}$, showing that the distribution of energy and momentum determines only the Ricci tensor, hence constraining the metric without determining it.[5] However, the metric does not determine which matter fields contribute to energy and momentum, or how they contribute.

To represent matter more explicitly in GR, one must supplement the pure gravitational models with mathematical fields and with rules for how the fields and their interactions contribute to T_{ab}. (If one writes T_{ab} as a sum of tensor fields that depend on the fields representing matter, the interaction terms are those that depend nontrivially on more than one field.) If the matter theories have a Lagrangian formulation, then the associated action principle determines their contributions to energy–momentum and their equations of motion (although nothing in GR requires that matter theories have a Lagrangian formulation).[6] These equations of motion sometimes invoke further spacetime structure χ – fields that do not themselves contribute to energy–momentum – such as frame fields or a temporal or spatial orientation. The fields in χ are often tensor fields on M, but more generally they can be sections of any principal bundle over M. Importantly, for every $p \in M$, each field takes on a value in its bundle's fiber over p, representing a sort of *part* of the field. This further justifies interpreting p as an atomic event, for it is the event of point-coincidence (or, perhaps better, *part*-coincidence) of matter fields at p.

In addition to the durations, lengths, and derived quantities assigned to events, the metric also assigns empirical content to the tensor fields in the pure gravitational models and to matter fields represented as tensor fields. It does so through an intermediary, the local orthonormal frame field. Such a field is a

---

[5] Perhaps surprisingly, these relationships depend on the four-dimensionality of spacetime; what, exactly, the field equation is supposed to be for other dimensions (if this is even a meaningful question) is subtle (Fletcher et al. 2018).

[6] One can also derive Eq. (1) from a Lagrangian formulation with the Einstein–Hilbert action (Hawking & Ellis 1973, 75), but this will not play a role in my subsequent discussion.

local assignment of four pointwise orthogonal vector fields, one timelike and the rest spacelike. Being "normal" here means having magnitude 1 according to the metric, so these vector fields express, respectively, one temporal or spatial unit.[7] Since they span the tangent space, any component of a tensor field at a point can be expressed as scalar multiples of tensor products of the frame elements. This scalar expresses the magnitude of the corresponding component in the temporal or spatial units chosen.

Aside from matter *fields*, it is also common to consider relativistic spacetimes with certain types of material *point particles*, the treatment of which further supports the interpretation of each $p \in M$ as an atomic event or material coincidence. This treatment adds three representational principles:

Histories The images of smooth timelike curves represent one-to-one the possible histories of massive *test* particles. (The curve producing such an image is called the corresponding particle's *worldline*.)

Freedom The images of smooth timelike *geodesic* curves represent one-to-one the possible histories of *force-free* massive test particles. (This principle is sometimes called the *geodesic principle*.)

Light The images of smooth null geodesic curves represent one-to-one the possible histories of (test) *light rays* (or *photons*, quantum connotations notwithstanding) in vacuum.

These principles invoke some terms to explicate. First, although they invoke the *histories* of particles, these principles are not restricted to spacetimes with a temporal orientation. Without one, there is no matter of fact represented about the correct narrative direction of a history. Second, a *test* particle (whether massive or light) is one whose mass does *not* contribute to T_{ab}. Their histories are affected by the curvature of the spacetime geometry, but not vice versa. Combined with **Duration**, **Histories** implies that the magnitude of a test particle's worldline is the duration of its history. Third, a curve $\gamma : I \to M$ is a *geodesic* when its tangent vector field v^a satisfies the geodesic equation, $v^a \nabla_a v^b = \mathbf{0}$, which states that the tangent vector field is constant along γ or, equivalently, that the (four-)acceleration $v^a \nabla_a v^b$ of the curve vanishes. Fourth, the *free* particles are those that are free of net force. Thus, **Freedom** is the four-dimensional general relativistic analogue of Newton's first law. The analogue of Newton's second law states that the net (four-)force F^a satisfies $F^a = m v^a \nabla_a v^b$, where m is the particle's mass. Fifth, that **Light** refers to histories of light rays in *vacuum* means only that the light rays do not interact with matter at the events of their histories, for example, so as to undergo refraction. They behave *as if* they were the only material system under consideration.

---

[7] One can justify this as a limiting-case extension of **Duration** and **Length**.

Sixth, each of these representational principles describes *possible* rather than actual histories. In a pure gravitational model, each appropriate curve image is a representational candidate that can be added explicitly to the model to make it more representationally complete.

For reasons I detail more fully in Sections 2.2 and 4.1, test particles occupy a liminal position in the structure of GR. So, stipulating principles about them adds unnecessary precariousness to the theory's interpretation – even more so if these, *rather* than **Duration** and **Length**, are taken as the theory's basic representational stipulations, as some authors do. Nevertheless, versions of these principles may be derived in special cases from **Duration**, **Length**, and particular matter theories, such as electromagnetism. Consequently, my partial interpretation does not adopt these as stipulations, but does invoke them on occasion in clearly applicable circumstances.[8]

In sum, while the minimal, "pure" gravitational models of GR are Lorentzian manifolds (M, g), the models more fully include the cosmological constant Λ, further auxiliary spacetime structure χ (such as a temporal or spatial orientation), and matter fields Φ (including, perhaps, test particles): $(M, g, \Lambda, \chi, \Phi)$. Applied to sets of events, as well as the components of tensor fields with respect to local frames, durations, lengths, and quantities derived from these are the empirical content of the models. Different models may nevertheless have different types of auxiliary spacetime structure and matter fields. For example, one model may have a scalar matter field and no auxiliary spacetime structure, while another may have a vector matter field and a temporal orientation. In any case, each of χ and Φ is or can be represented as a field or fields over M. Mathematically, two models, $(M, g, \Lambda, \chi, \Phi)$ and $(M', g', \Lambda', \chi', \Phi')$, are isomorphic when there is a diffeomorphism $\psi : M \to M'$ that preserves all of the structure of these models, that is, $\Lambda = \Lambda'$ and its pullback ψ^* satisfies $\psi^*(g') = g$, $\psi^*(\chi') = \chi$, and $\psi^*(\Phi') = \Phi$.[9] Isomorphic models have the same representational capacities, meaning that they can represent the same states of affairs equally well, because the representational principles refer only to the structures of the models. In particular, isomorphic models can represent the same empirical content equally well.

Alluding to "concrete" interpretations like the foregoing, Curiel (2009, 47n3) writes that "[o]ne can fairly argue over the virtues and demerits of each with

---

[8] Readers familiar with GR may note that many other "physical principles" besides the ones I have discussed have figured importantly in the history of relativity theory. I set these aside for lack of space and their superfluousness for articulating my partial interpretation.

[9] For matter fields valued outside of products of the tangent and cotangent space at a point, the structure-preservation conditions are more complicated, but eliding that subtlety is of little moment to the remainder.

respect to depth, rigor and thoroughness, and with respect to a whole set of particular philosophical problems and issues," while holding that they are nevertheless sufficiently clear, in contrast with the case of quantum theory. Such contrasts aside, I aim in the remaining sections of this Element to amplify the foregoing interpretation by more thoroughly and rigorously treating (1) what *possibilities* GR represents, (2) the *internal structure* of those possibilities and their interrelations, and, to some extent, (3) how those possibilities *differ* from what's come before, for example, from special relativity and Newtonian gravitation. To my knowledge, such a comprehensive interpretation of GR has not been recently attempted. I hope that readers will use my interpretation as a foil in their own work, either to amplify parts not yet sufficiently thorough and rigorous or to propose contrasting interpretations. In a word, I hope that it will engender further *fair arguing* over our best theory of space, time, and gravitation.

2 How and What Relativistic Spacetimes Represent

2.1 Two Views on Representation

In Section 1, I adumbrated an interpretation of GR by stipulating what certain of the mathematical elements in the models represent. This enables one of the core functions of modeling: facilitating surrogative reasoning. In reasoning about the models – Lorentzian manifolds, perhaps with extra structure – we arrive at conclusions about what the models represent, ways that a gravitational universe, or part of one, could be. Like with other parts of science, this often involves idealization. In addition to abstracting away or simplifying the properties represented, sometimes one represents one sort of phenomena *as* another (Frigg & Nguyen 2021, §7). For instance, one may represent extended but localized events *as* an atomic event in spacetime or represent a part of a universe *as* a whole one. Examples of the latter typically include asymptotically flat spacetimes used in gravitational wave modeling (cf. Section 4.4), where the gravitational wave detector is "at infinity" outside the model.[10] There are, of course, many other important questions about the nature of scientific representation, and even more competing detailed answers thereto (Frigg & Nguyen 2021). But like with the examples of localized events and (non-)cosmological models just discussed, this interpretation of GR does not demand anything more of scientific representation than that for other typical scientific theories.

---

[10] Such a model is inextendible, meaning that any embedding of it into another spacetime model is an isomorphism. Being inextendible is arguably sufficient for a model to represent a universe, rather than a proper part of it, as the model cannot be extended to include the other parts.

There may be another interpretation, or program for interpretation, of GR that *does* demand more. On this reading, the "dynamical" approach or perspective of Harvey Brown (2005), elaborating suggestions by Eddington (1965, 146) and Anderson (1967, 342), insists in particular that the metric g can represent durations, lengths, and other geometrical facts if and only if it correlates appropriately with the behavior of material clocks and rigid rods. (This is not intended as a reductive definition, as time and distance are implicit in what it means for a physical system to be a clock or rod.) One establishes this correlation, Brown and colleagues suggest, in a two-step justification (cf. Read et al. 2018, §4.1). First, one does so in special relativity, where one argues that the Minkowski metric η is merely a codification of and reduces to the dynamical symmetries of matter, including clocks and rods (Brown & Pooley 2001, 2006). Second, one assumes the *strong equivalence principle* (SEP) (Brown 2005, 8–9, 151, 170).[11] There are many formulations of the SEP, but in the present context it amounts to the claim that for any $p \in M$ of a relativistic spacetime (M,g), there is a neighborhood of p and inertial coordinates (determined by g) thereon, according to which the metric g approximately takes the form of η and the equations of motion for matter fields approximately take on their special relativistic form (cf. Fletcher & Weatherall 2023a,b). One then interprets the metric g locally and approximately as one would the Minkowski metric η. Since η is correlated with the readings of clocks and measures of rigid rods in special relativity, so too must g, locally and approximately.

This alternative strategy is striking, but it faces challenges at every step of its execution and justification. First, it is not yet clear *why* the successful representation of physical magnitudes ought to meet a different standard in GR than in other, generic scientific modeling contexts. Rugh and Zinkernagel (2009, 2017), arguing for a similar thesis regarding time, assert that some material process in a spacetime region needs to set a timescale in order for one to represent time in that region. This is because the constants appearing in the EFE, c and G, do not set a timescale themselves. However, they are mistaken that this is a necessary condition: Particular solutions to the EFE can well determine a timescale even if the EFE do not, and if the cosmological constant Λ is nonzero, it sets timescales and length scales in concert with c. In any case, fixing a timescale is not necessary for representing time – rather, it *presupposes* that time is already represented in a model, only with the unit for time unfixed.

One might instead justify a different standard in cases in which the targets of the model are obscure, as is the case arguably in quantum mechanics and

---

[11] Brown (2005, 9) also assumes versions of **Duration** and **Length**, which I only discuss further in the following subsection since they drop out of later discussions (e.g., Read et al. 2018).

quantum gravity (Curiel 2009, §§5–6). But the targets in GR are familiar, quantitative concepts of duration and length, and concepts derivative from them. They are no more obscure in GR than they are in other spacetime theories. In reply, Brown (2005, 8, 150) might emphasize that only in GR is the metric, which is to represent these concepts, "a dynamical agent" that interacts with matter. Read et al. (2018, §2.2) clarify that this means that the metric is not a fixed field in the models of GR, and it enters ineliminably into the EFE. This is true, but from it nothing about standards for representation with this field follows. Nothing about spatiotemporal concepts obscures how non-fixed fields could represent them.

Brown (2005, 160, 175) and Read et al. (2018, §6) also correctly observe, using examples from alternative gravitational theories, that a field cannot represent durations, lengths, and so on solely in virtue of its *mathematical* form. (Indeed, general doctrines about scientific representation that identify it with structural isomorphism face similar, grave difficulties [Frigg & Nguyen 2021 §4.2].) However, they seem to conflate this formalist or structuralist position regarding representation with any in which "the metric field has a *primitive* [i.e., unanalyzed] connection to spacetime geometry." That the interpretation of Section 1 does not explicate concepts of durations, lengths, and so on does not imply that they cannot, or should not, admit of further conceptual and operational analysis. But such analysis lies in fundamental metrology's province, not GR's.

The second challenge targets the first step of the justification, that in special relativity the Minkowski metric is reduced to a codification of the dynamical symmetries of matter, including rods and clocks. As Norton (2008) and Hagar and Hemmo (2013) argue, these sorts of justification must fail if they do not already assume some primitive spatiotemporal concepts. The underlying idea is simply that describing the dynamics of matter, or interpreting abstract equations as representing matter and its change over time, presupposes the representation of the very spatiotemporal concepts under consideration. Pooley (2013, 572) and Myrvold (2019, §6) concede on behalf of the dynamical approach that they must represent some spatiotemporal concepts in order to secure the justification in question, emphasizing that this is nonetheless acceptable for some of their ontological claims about the reducibility of the Minkowski metric or the explanation of its symmetries (for more on which, see Section 3). However, it amounts to abandonment of the stronger demand for what it takes to represent durations, lengths, and so on.

The third challenge targets the second step that applies the interpretation of the Minkowski metric η – the second challenge notwithstanding – locally to the interpretation of the general spacetime metric g. This step infers the interpretation of g from the approximate, local coincidence of symmetry groups of equations involving η and g, but it is not clear why this step is valid. After all, as discussed before in this section, the *mathematical* properties of an object in a model do not determine anything about what the object represents. It seems rather that a spatiotemporal interpretation of g must be presupposed in order to infer that this mathematical coincidence has representational significance, but this is to presuppose the very fact to be established. Moreover, there is no logical relationship between symmetries of equations governing matter fields and spacetime symmetries, even of the approximate local sort (Fletcher 2020*a*), as would be needed in the two-step justification.

In light of these challenges, one might abandon the stronger requirement for what it takes for a representation to be of spatiotemporal concepts but still pursue Brown's two-step process in interpreting GR. Ehlers (1973, 45) considers this option, remarking that it is still not "theoretically completely satisfactory" without elaborating on why. Nevertheless, one can adduce at least four reasons:

1. It is circular. The third challenge showed that the second step of the process must presuppose facts about how g represents durations and lengths in order to justify why the local matching of the structure of g with that of η has any interpretational significance.
2. It is doubly vague. First, because the interpretation relies on an approximate rather than an exact matching of metric structure and matter dynamics in a local region, it is unclear to what extent its validity depends on the precise notion of approximation and its degree. Different notions of approximation will in general be incompatible with one another (Fletcher & Weatherall 2023*b*). Second, because there is no unique way to match locally and approximately the structure of g with that of η – there are infinitely many different ηs that will agree only at a point (Fletcher & Weatherall 2023*a*) – there is no unique degree to which the approximation holds.
3. It is doubly restricted. It only provides an interpretation of the local structure of spacetime, while certain global properties, such as those concerning causality (Section 5), are certainly of interpretational interest. It also restricts the possible matter models to those that satisfy the SEP, relative to the notion and degree of approximation chosen.
4. It conflicts with some of our explanatory expectations. By interpreting GR through the lens of the less encompassing, accurate, and fundamental special theory of relativity, it seems to conflict with the common expectation that the order of interpretation (if any) should be in the other direction, from more fundamental to less. Rather than explaining the success of special relativistic physics, such success is seemingly guaranteed by interpretational postulate.

In this way, the two-step interpretational strategy is similar to Bohr's employment of "classical concepts" in the basis of his interpretation of quantum mechanics (Faye 2019) and is vulnerable to analogous criticisms.

None of these reasons is decisive; we may well accept an interpretation of a theory with each of these vices if there is no better on offer. But the interpretation of Section 1 suffers from none of these vices, in addition to being much simpler and easier to apply.

There is nonetheless an important insight within the original demand to connect representations of duration and length with material models of clocks and rods. To see why, suppose that instead of **Duration** and **Lengths**, I had chosen the following simpler, absurd alternatives:

No Duration The duration of any collection of events is 0.
No Length The length of any collection of events is 0.

I am of course free to stipulate these representational principles. But if I were to do so, I would find that the resulting models misrepresent systematically: Essentially any case of spacetime modeling of interest will involve representing durations and lengths well above zero. This may move me to revise my models and – especially in this case, in light of the *pattern* of misrepresentation – my representational principles of the models' targets. The defeasible process of testing and adjusting models and representational principles against empirical and theoretical evidence about the target phenomena, so as to arrive at a reflective equilibrium, however temporary, until new evidence arrives, supports the equilibrium commitments over others considered (Daniels 2020).

Even when there are no other potentially suitable representational principles explicitly under consideration, one might wonder how much this is just due to a lack of imagination. If stipulated representational principles can be (in part) responsible for misrepresentation, then how can one be confident that one's adopted principles don't contribute to misrepresentation in some subtle, systematic way? There are at least three strategies for coordinating representation and phenomena with models.

1. **Prediction.** The extensive successful predictions of and control with a theory, using its representational principles, provides some inductive evidence at least for the models successfully applied. General relativity has passed all such applications in which it clearly applies, as of this writing.
2. **Accommodation.** When the models of a theory accommodate or closely approximate the descriptions and predictions of the models of a successfully applied prior theory (including its representational principles) to a common target, it provides abductive evidence also for those models. Most commonly

for GR, these prior theories are the special theory of relativity and Newtonian gravitation.

3. **Examples.** We may construct simple, paradigmatic examples within models of the theories, and examples that we have largely independent reasons to believe should illustrate or instantiate the representational target. (They might be regarded as thought experiments [Brown & Fehige 2022], the role of simplicity in which is only to exclude inessential distractions.) In the case of GR, these targets would be durations, lengths, and concepts derived from them.

The last two strategies for gleaning evidence of the adequacy of representational principles, **Accommodation** and **Examples**, resemble Brown's requirements for justifying why the metric g can represent spatiotemporal quantities. But these strategies do not serve to make the metric's representation of durations and lengths possible or apt, as Brown seems to demand: One can perfectly well stipulate how the metric represents these targets, as I have done in Section 1. Instead, these strategies, when successful, merely provide evidence that the principles do not contribute to systematic misrepresentation. I turn to some of this evidence, and other connections between the representational principles of GR, in the next subsection.

2.2 The Representation of Kinematical Properties

What evidence do we have that **Duration** does not lead GR into systematic misrepresentations? At the least, we have the sorts of evidence that **Prediction** and **Accommodation** afford: inductive evidence from the successful application of GR in tasks that depend on precise timing, such as in GPS systems (Ashby 2003), and abductive evidence from the approximate matching of the representation of durations in Newtonian gravitation (Fletcher 2019) and special relativity (Fletcher & Weatherall 2023*b*). But both of these could be challenged: Perhaps the duration of a timelike curve γ is best represented by a quantity that diverges from $|\gamma|$ in circumstances we have not examined, such as in high accelerations (Mainwaring & Stedman 1993, Mashhoon 2017) or strong ambient matter fields (Hojman 2018). Rindler (1960, 28–30) observes, for instance, that representing the duration of γ as being independent of its acceleration is only the syntactically simplest extension of the formula that applies in less controversial cases where its acceleration vanishes.

Syntactic simplicity, however, is not always the mark of truth or accuracy. This is in part why I, in previous work, pursued **Examples** by constructing models of light clocks in an arbitrary relativistic spacetime (Fletcher 2013). For a given timelike curve, I showed how to construct an infinite sequence of "companion" timelike curves that in a precise sense converge to the given curve. These curves represent idealized mirrors, between which bounces a null geodesic, representing a light ray. As the companion curves converge, the construction "measures" the magnitude of any closed segment of the given curve, as accurately and regularly as one wishes, in terms of the number of bounces and a certain measure of the distance d between the given curve and its companion. If one assumes that such constructions are paradigmatic clocks, then one should represent the duration of a timelike curve by its magnitude. In other words, if arbitrarily small light clocks are ideal clocks, measuring duration perfectly, then one should adopt **Duration**. This is why **Duration** is often called the *clock hypothesis* and is stated in terms of ideal clocks (that they measure the magnitudes of curves). (Some state the clock hypothesis merely in terms of the *independence* of the rate of an ideal clock from acceleration, but such statements are incomplete because they do not fix the duration of γ as $|\gamma|$.) Other interpretive principles support, but do not establish, that light clocks are paradigmatic clocks: **Light** establishes what the bouncing null curve represents, and **Length** justifies why the numerical quantity d represents a length. Light clocks' simplicity is an interpretive virtue: complex constructions that represent actual clock mechanisms better may fail to be ideal because of how they are engineered.

The logic of this construction is important for its interpretation. It does not state that, for any standard of accuracy and regularity, there is a light clock of a single size that measures the magnitude of (any closed segment of) any timelike curve to those standards. Rather, the size of the clock needed is bespoke to the curve: For any standard of accuracy and regularity and (any closed segment of) any timelike curve, there is sufficiently small light clock that measures its magnitude to those standards: In short, the order of the last two quantifiers is reversed. It is thus compatible with the claim that "for any given clock, no matter how ideal its behaviour when moving inertially, there will in principle be an acceleration such that to achieve it the external force acting on the clock will disrupt its inner workings" (Brown 2018, 54). It is not any individual light clock that is ideal, but the entire family of them working in concert. There is no need to demand one clock to rule them all. Thus, I would deny that, as Knox (2010) and Brown (2018) respectively suggest, the clock hypothesis *fails* for certain neutrino oscillation systems and for accelerated iron atoms and muons. Rather, the analysis of these systems merely shows their periodic behavior or their decay rates cannot serve as ideal clocks under certain conditions.

Another sort of response to my results has been to question the adequacy of **Light**, which I used as part of the support for the premise that light clocks are paradigmatic clocks. Menon et al. (2020, §4.3) point out that in a variably dispersive or refractive medium, the worldlines of light rays may not effectively have the same relative velocity to a timelike worldline (representing a mirror in the light clock), so that in such contexts null geodesics are not adequate representations of light. Just so, but there is a sense in which this objection misunderstands both **Light** and the structure of **Examples**.

Light is a representational principle for test light rays in vacuum, which are limits of certain solutions to Maxwell's electromagnetic field equations. That they are test light rays means that their energy and momentum do not contribute to T_{ab} in the EFE; that they are "in vacuum" means not that $T_{ab} = \mathbf{0}$ at the events they are present, but rather that they do not interact with any dispersive or refractive material medium. Thus, objecting to **Light** on the basis of dispersion or refraction, if one accepts test light rays in vacuum in this sense, is simply to conflate such rays with ones not in vacuum.

There seems to be little room in the practice of the general relativist not to permit test light rays in vacuum. While I affirm that test matter requires more delicate treatment than it is usually given, there are coherent and fruitful treatments. But to the extent that, as I discuss more in Section 4.1, it is an approximation of the behavior matter that we expect to be realized in the best general relativistic models of portions of our universe, one might hold the assumption that light clocks are paradigmatic clocks to be less plausible. The simplicity of the light clock, in other words, may turn from virtue to vice if it is too extreme. One can ameliorate this softened version of the objection, if admitted, by providing an entirely analogous construction that allows the bouncing light ray or particle to have a variable speed in the inter-mirror medium, which can either be varying sufficiently slowly (Fletcher 2013, 1382n9) or for which one merely corrects with a more complicated limiting formula. It is immaterial whether light is the periodic mechanism.

Before returning to the other representational principles about test matter – **Histories** and **Freedom** – at the end of this subsection, I focus attention on **Length** and then briefly on other representational principles derived from or supported by it and **Duration**.

From the beginning of relativity theory (Einstein 1923/1905), rigid measuring rods have often been invoked in the same breath as lengths, just as clocks have with duration (see Brown 2005, 4 et passim.). If one wishes to pursue **Examples** for **Length**, then one might begin in analogy with **Duration** by analyzing a simple, paradigmatic model of rods. (Of course, both **Prediction** and **Accommodation** are also available.) But one would be quickly frustrated: There is no completely satisfactory concept of rigidity for an extended object in relativity theory, as the best option, Born rigidity, precludes any acceleration (Synge 1960, Ch. III.5). Moreover, it is less obvious whether it is possible to define any concept of rigidity at all without already presupposing that the magnitudes of spacelike curves represent lengths – for what is rigidity if not the constancy of all spatial relations between parts? Even without rigidity, it is not entirely obvious how to define uniquely the length of an object in relativity theory, as several definitions that are equivalent in prerelativistic physics are not in GR (Geroch 1978, 140–150). Synge (1960, 108) goes so far as to deny the need for an additional representational principle like **Length** at all: "*For us time is the only basic measure.* Length (or distance), in so far as it is necessary or desirable to introduce it, is strictly a derived concept." Synge (1960, Ch. III.4) goes on to define the length of a spacelike vector in terms of that of timelike and null vectors, but it is unclear if this really serves to eliminate or reduce length concepts to time concepts for spacelike curves.

It may yet be possible to fulfill Synge's ambition through some conceptual and technical ingenuity, but I shall take an intermediate position here by sketching a construction that assumes **Duration**, **Light**, and (perhaps eliminably) **Freedom**. Instead of using rods, it uses radar (light) ranging of distant events (Geroch 1978, Chs. 5–6), much as Einstein (1923/1905) originally proposed, but inspired by the discussion of Synge (1960, Ch. III.12). (One can well dispense with Einstein's rods and refer only to the events where light is incident on their ends.) Given a spacelike curve, construct a sequence of timelike geodesics intersecting and normal to it with the following property: Each geodesic (except for the last) has a pair of null geodesics, representing light rays, connecting an event on its past and an event on its future to the event where the next timelike geodesic intersects the spacelike curve. The sum of the durations of these timelike curve segments in between the light emission and reception is proportional to an estimate of the distances between the events where these timelike curves intersect the spacelike curve. As this sequence grows in number and its elements closer together, the quantity proportional to this sum converges to the magnitude of the length of the curve. Insofar as this radar ranging method for distances is a paradigmatic construction for determining distances, we should represent the latter according to **Length**.

I conjecture that the details of this construction can be filled out to give a justification of **Length** based on **Duration**, **Light**, and perhaps **Freedom** that is as satisfactory as the one I gave for **Duration** in terms of **Length** and **Light**. (I am untroubled by a coherentist justification for representational principles in which some support others and vice versa – cf. what Weatherall [2017] calls the "puzzleball" view of physical theories.) Aside from **Length**, one could engage in similar projects for justifying our usual representations of angle and relative velocity (Synge 1960, Ch. III.6–7), energy and momentum (Synge 1960, Ch. IV), rotation (Malament 2012, Ch. 3.2–3), and much else.

Notably, many of these derived quantities are *relational* to some auxiliary spacetime structure or material field, such as a particular frame field or a coordinate system defined by such a field. It is sometimes expressed that frame- or coordinate-dependent quantities are not meaningful in GR. For, if one omits the auxiliary structure in the expression of a spacetime model, such quantities might not seem to be invariant under isomorphisms. But once such structure is included, it too must be pulled back along the diffeomorphism giving rise to the isomorphism. So such denials of meaning can be more charitably interpreted as denials of the representational significance, or at the least the fundamentality, in some sense, of the auxiliary structure on which these quantities depend. (See also my discussion of energy–momentum pseudotensors in Sections 4.3–4.4.)

Finally, both **Histories** and **Freedom** deserve a brief special discussion. They are both representational principles for test particles, but there is something dubious about test matter. As I discuss more in Section 4.1, all realistic matter fields – ones that are at least in the neighborhood of being satisfactory representations of matter in our actual universe – contribute to T_{ab}, unlike test matter. We allow test matter into our ontology only because it is an approximation of matter with relatively meager energy and momentum; we allow particles into our ontology only because they are an approximation of matter that is relatively localized.[12]

Given this, "What should we make of a foundational principle that, by the lights of the theory of which it is part, relies on the counterfactual behavior of impossible objects?" (Weatherall 2020*a*, 222). That our interest in test particles is thus only derivative suggests that **Histories**, **Freedom**, and **Light** should be derivative, too, from more fundamental principles about matter fields, namely their equations of motion and contributions to energy–momentum.

Since almost the advent of GR in 1915, there have been attempts to derive **Freedom** in particular from other assumptions (Brown 2005, 162). I confine my discussion to some recent developments and refer to the citations therein and to Weatherall (2020*a*) for broader reviews. Geroch and Weatherall (2018) show **Freedom** follows from a few assumptions: The matter fields under consideration are source-free, and their associated energy–momentum T_{ab} satisfies the **conservation** condition, $\nabla_a T^{ab} = 0$, and the **dominant energy condition (DEC)**: For every timelike vector v^a at any event, $T_{ab}v^a v^b \geq 0$ and $T^b_a v^a$ is timelike or null. I discuss the interpretation of **DEC** in Section 4.1, but the first two conditions simply state, respectively, that the field is not undergoing any external forces and is not interacting with any other matter

---

[12] See Weatherall (2020*a*, §2.1) for some of the problems with non-test particles as distributional sources for the EFE; see Fletcher (2020*c*) for problems for **Histories** in spacetimes with closed timelike curves.

fields. This is exactly what one should expect of *free* particles. Moreover, Geroch and Weatherall (2018) prove **Histories** for Maxwell's equations *with* sources. None of these results require the EFE, so it appears that similar results extend to many other spacetime theories, even nonrelativistic ones (Weatherall 2017, 2019).

2.3 Einstein's Field Equation and the Cosmological Constant

As I mentioned in Section 1, the EFE, Eq. (1), correlates curvature at an event with the energy and momentum at that event. In Section 3.2, when I turn to the nature of the determination and dependence relations between spacetime structure and matter, it will be helpful to know more about *how* they correlate and depend on one another. For this purpose, we can adapt some of the representational insights of the previous subsection to express two distinct characterizations of the meaning of the EFE in terms of orthonormal frames. (For these characterizations, I adapt the treatment by Malament [2012, 162–166].)

One expression of the meaning of the EFE concerns the geometry of *space* relative to every observer at an event $p \in M$. Represent the observer with an orthonormal frame $\{\overset{i}{e}{}^a\}$ at p with timelike component $\overset{0}{e}{}^a$. Consider any spacelike hypersurface S intersecting p, with vanishing extrinsic curvature, whose tangent vectors there are spanned by the spacelike components of the frame. (To say that it has vanishing extrinsic curvature means that every geodesic of the hypersurface, considered as a metric submanifold, is a geodesic of (M, g).) Such a hypersurface represents any construction of space at p for the observer that is *standard* at p. The subset of these consisting of *geodesically generated* hypersurfaces, whose events are composed from those of the spacelike geodesics through p, are those that are standard on every point on which they are defined. Now let $\mathcal{R}_S$ denote the scalar curvature of S at p. The EFE holds at p if and only if for all such frames $\{\overset{i}{e}{}^a\}$ and surfaces S,

$$\mathcal{R}_S = \frac{16\pi G}{c^4} T_{ab}\overset{0}{e}{}^a\overset{0}{e}{}^b + 2\Lambda. \tag{3}$$

Since $T_{ab}\overset{0}{e}{}^a\overset{0}{e}{}^b$ is the energy density at p according to the observer, this equivalence states that the scalar curvature of space for any observer is an increasing linear function of the energy density that the observer would ideally measure. The cosmological constant Λ determines the function's intercept. In case it seems remarkable that the EFE can be characterized using only energy density, since T_{ab} also describes momentum, recall that this equivalence constrains the energy densities as ideally measured by *all* observers: The momentum flux observed for some becomes energy for others.

The second expression of the meaning of the EFE concerns the relative acceleration between free observers. Consider now not just a single observer with an orthonormal frame but a frame field $\{\overset{i}{e}{}^{a}\}$ on an open set of spacetime, again with timelike component $\overset{0}{e}{}^{a}$, but whose integral curves are timelike geodesics. The spacelike components, $\overset{i}{e}{}^{a}$ for $i \in \{1,2,3\}$, are *connecting fields* that designate the direction of neighboring integral curves. Further suppose that on at least one of the integral curves γ, the Lie derivative of these spacelike components with respect to the timelike component vanishes, that is, $\pounds_{\overset{0}{e}} \overset{i}{e}{}^{a} = 0$ for $i \in \{1,2,3\}$. Then $\overset{0}{e}{}^{a}\nabla_{a}(\overset{0}{e}{}^{b}\nabla_{b}\overset{i}{e}{}^{c})$ represents the relative acceleration of integral curves with γ in the direction $\overset{i}{e}{}^{a}$. Call the average of the radial components of these relative accelerations at a point p – the components respectively parallel to $\{\overset{i}{e}{}^{a}\}$ – *the average radial acceleration* (ARA) at p. The EFE holds at p if and only if for all such geodesic frame fields $\{\overset{i}{e}{}^{a}\}$ on a neighborhood of p,

$$\text{ARA} = -\frac{8\pi G}{3c^2}\left(T_{ab} - \frac{1}{2}Tg_{ab}\right)\overset{0}{e}{}^{a}\overset{0}{e}{}^{b} + \frac{\Lambda c^2}{3}. \tag{4}$$

Negative values of ARA indicate that gravitation is attractive, in the sense that on average nearby freely falling observers will accelerate towards one another in their frames of reference.

To get another sense for the meaning of Eq. (4), it can be helpful to specialize to a perfect fluid model (cf. Baez & Bunn 2005). In this case, supposing that the frame field is comoving with the fluid, $T_{ab} = \rho\overset{0}{e}{}_{a}\overset{0}{e}{}_{b} + \sum_{i=1}^{3}\overset{i}{p}\overset{i}{e}{}_{a}\overset{i}{e}{}_{b}$, where ρ is the energy density of the fluid and $\overset{i}{p}$ is the fluid's pressure in the direction $\overset{i}{e}{}^{a}$. The fluid has a volume function $V = \epsilon_{abcd}\overset{0}{e}{}^{a}\overset{1}{e}{}^{b}\overset{2}{e}{}^{c}\overset{3}{e}{}^{d}$, where ϵ_{abcd} is a volume element defined in a neighborhood of p. Then $3(\text{ARA}) = [\overset{0}{e}{}^{a}\nabla_{a}(\overset{0}{e}{}^{b}\nabla_{b}V)]/V \equiv \ddot{V}/V$, and

$$\frac{\ddot{V}}{V} = -4\pi G\left(\rho + \frac{1}{c^2}\sum_{i=1}^{3}\overset{i}{p}\right) + \Lambda c^2. \tag{5}$$

Thus, the EFE holds at p if and only if the change in the rate of change of volume, per unit volume, is proportional to the sum of the energy density at p, the pressures in three orthogonal spatial directions at p, and the cosmological constant.

One can gain further insight by combining Eq. (3) and Eq. (4). This yields that the EFE holds at p if and only if

$$\text{ARA} = \frac{4\pi G}{3c^2}T - \frac{\mathcal{R}_S c^2}{6} + \frac{2\Lambda c^2}{3}. \tag{6}$$

The EFE evidently demands a certain algebraic balance at every event between ARA of geodesic reference frames and a weighted combination of energy, momentum, scalar spatial curvature, and the cosmological constant. Eq. (6) is in turn equivalent to the pair of equations

$$(8\pi G/c^4)T = -R - 4\Lambda, \tag{7}$$

$$\text{ARA} = -(R + \mathcal{R}_S)c^2/6, \tag{8}$$

where (again) Eq. (7) is the trace of the EFE, which substituted into Eq. (6) yields Eq. (8). Remarkably, as this latter equation shows, the aforementioned balance can be cast entirely in local geometrical terms – without reference to energy or the cosmological constant – as being proportional to the average of the spatial and spatiotemporal scalar curvatures there. This equation alone is implied by but does not imply the EFE, however, as it determines nothing about how curvature and acceleration are correlated with matter and the cosmological constant. But it turns out that only the trace of the EFE, Eq. (7), is needed to provide this correlation.

So far, I have discussed the meaning of the EFE while leaving tacit that of the cosmological constant. Einstein brought attention to the possibility of the term Λg_{ab} in the EFE in 1917 to allow GR to model a certain static cosmological model, one in which the universe described is neither expanding nor contracting. He selected the sign of Λ to counterbalance the attractive nature of gravitation without it. He then abandoned it by the early 1930s when (among other reasons) observational evidence indicated that in fact the universe was expanding. Since then, astronomers and cosmologists have repeatedly reenacted variations on this theme as they attempt to reconcile cosmological models with observation. (See Ray [1990], Earman [2001], and O'Raifeartaigh et al. [2018] for more details of this history of justifications for introducing or discarding the constant.)

Despite its chequered history, the cosmological constant currently plays a central role in modern cosmology's standard model, called the ΛCDM (or concordance) model (Smeenk 2013). ("CDM" is an abbreviation for "cold dark matter.") The current best estimates for Λ give it a definitely nonnegative, but small, value (Aghanim et al. 2020). Its most straightforward interpretation is as a new constant of nature that, if nonzero, sets an intrinsic length scale – hence, with c, an intrinsic timescale – to pure gravitational models. Eqs. (3)–(7) detail what this scale means for local spatial geometry, ARA, and so on. For instance, at events with an effective vacuum, meaning that $T_{ab} = \mathbf{0}$, a nonzero Λ ensures a correspondingly nonzero spatial curvature and ARA. This role as a constant, dimensionful (length^{-2}) number coheres with its representation as such in the Einstein-Hilbert action.

I will return to the relationship between Λ and an effective vacuum shortly. But first I turn to a different sense in which Λ could be a "constant," with alleged implications for the possible models of GR. Substituting Eq. (7) into the EFE (Eq. (1)) to eliminate Λ yields the "trace-free" EFE,

$$R_{ab} - \frac{1}{4}Rg_{ab} = \frac{8\pi G}{c^4}\left(T_{ab} - \frac{1}{4}Tg_{ab}\right). \tag{9}$$

This equation is not equivalent with the EFE, but when combined with any one of the following three equations, it is:

$$\nabla_a T^{ab} = \mathbf{0}, \tag{10}$$

$$\nabla_a[(8\pi G/c^4)T + R] = \mathbf{0}, \tag{11}$$

$$(8\pi G/c^4)T + R = \text{const.} \tag{12}$$

The point of this reformulation is that one can rewrite the EFE in terms of equations that eliminate reference to Λ. In fact, it can be recovered by labeling the constant in Eq. (12) as -4Λ, in which case the equation just becomes Eq. (7).

Earman (2003, 563) writes of this reformulation that "it is not a new universal constant of nature but rather a humble constant of integration" so that, *unlike* the standard formulation, "the value of [Λ] can vary from solution to solution (in the philosophers' jargon, from physically possible world to physically possible world)" (Earman 2003, 562). (Earman [2003, 562] also considers, implicitly, another reformulation in which the cosmological "constant" is not a number but a scalar field λ that satisfies the field equation $\nabla_a\lambda = \mathbf{0}$. Then, presumably, λ would be just a "humble" scalar field. Remarks analogous to mine in the rest of this section about constants apply mutatis mutandis to such fields.)

Whether this comparative conclusion follows depends on what further assumptions one is willing to make. On my reconstruction, Earman implicitly assumes the following two premises:

1. A dimensionful constant associated with a physical theory appears in the theory's fundamental laws if and only if it is a universal constant of nature.
2. A dimensionful constant associated with a theory is a universal constant of nature if and only if it takes on only one value in the theory's models.

The first premise is needed to conclude that some constants, such as c, are universal constants of nature, and that others, such as λ (as a "humble constant of integration"), are not. The second premise is needed to conclude that this division entails a difference in the possible values the constants can take on in the models of the theory. Each part of each conclusion employs one direction of each of the biconditionals.

There are good reasons to reject each of these premises. As I mentioned in Section 1 and discuss in more detail in Section 3.1, the mathematical formalism of a theory is only a guide to its interpretation. Any strict rule for correlating them, such as the first premise, can hold at best ceteris paribus. In this case, the ceteris are not paribus, for it conflicts with scientific practice. For instance, Earman (2003, 562) indicates the electron charge as an example of a constant of nature, but according to QED, this is only an effective quantity arising from the bare charge of the electron. The same goes for the mass of many of the fundamental particles. So there are constants of nature associated with a theory that do not appear in fundamental equations. Conversely, the quantity $8\pi G/c^4$ appears in all versions of the EFE, but it is not itself considered to be a fundamental constant, but an algebraic function of the constants of nature c and G.

The second premise also conflicts with scientific practice. Contrary to what Earman seems to suggest, it is very common for physicists to consider models with different values of physical constants as solutions to a physical theory (cf. Read 2023, 19n35). The principal interest of the models whose constants take on the actual values is that they, presumably, will be more descriptively and predictively accurate than those with different values, not because they are the only "true" models of the theory. Conversely, it is sometimes useful to restrict what one would otherwise have considered to be possible values of a quantity that is not a fundamental constant. For example, this was Sommerfeld's strategy, in introducing his quantization condition, for avoiding the ultraviolet catastrophe and recovering Nernst's law (Duncan & Janssen 2022).

So, there is no good reason to suppose that reformulating the EFE according to the outline of the previous few paragraphs automatically changes the range of values that Λ can take in the models of the theory. Proposals for wider or narrower ranges of values, which assert corresponding ranges of physical possibilities, are equally compatible with the standard EFE and these alternatives, such as the trace-free EFE with the conservation condition.

Nevertheless, these different proposals *do* suggest that the interpretation of Λ may be more or less *relatively fundamental*, in the sense that they may support the same possibilities for Λ while differing in what subjunctive (counterfactual) conditionals they support. In the standard EFE, Λ is not determined by any other constant, structure, or field. Consequently, as one varies T, for instance, Λ remains the same. But using the trace-free EFE plus conservation condition, Λ is determined by the values of T and R. Hence, as one varies T, Λ will in general vary, too. (I am setting aside how to implement the semantics for these dependencies in terms of conditionals, but see Fletcher [2021*a*] for a proposal.)

In Section 3.2, I will have much more to say about relations of determination and dependence in GR. Before doing so, I conclude this section with a quite different perspective on what Λ represents that has been influential in cosmology, and a "problem," or a research question, that it has engendered.

In the two characterizations of the EFE in terms of spatial curvature and ARA, Λ formally plays a similar role as energy and momentum, except that it does not vary from event to event. Indeed, one can formally rewrite the EFE simply by moving the cosmological constant term to the "matter" side from the "geometry" side:

$$R_{ab} - \frac{1}{2}Rg_{ab} = \frac{8\pi G}{c^4}T_{ab} + \Lambda g_{ab} = \frac{8\pi G}{c^4}\left(T_{ab} + \overset{\Lambda}{T}_{ab}\right), \tag{13}$$

where one has defined $\overset{\Lambda}{T}_{ab} = (\Lambda c^4/8\pi G)g_{ab}$. One then interprets T_{ab} not as the net energy–momentum tensor, but only that for ordinary, non-gravitational fields; $\overset{\Lambda}{T}_{ab}$ is the energy–momentum of the "gravitational field" g or of spacetime itself. Here, Λ is still a constant of nature, but quantifies the scale of gravitation's or spacetime's contribution to energy–momentum.

This interpretation ascribes energy–momentum to g or to events themselves, while the interpretation of Section 1 does so only to matter fields. I elaborate reasons to prefer the latter in Sections 3.3 and 4.1, where I discuss the ontology of the "gravitational field" and constraints on acceptable matter theories in terms of how they contribute to energy–momentum.

These reasons notwithstanding, if one assumes that a "vacuum" is a model of GR in which $T_{ab} = \mathbf{0}$, then $\overset{\Lambda}{T}_{ab}$ represents the local energy and momentum of such a vacuum. It is then extremely tempting to identify this "energy of the vacuum" with the "vacuum energy" of quantum field theory, that is, the expected energy of the ground state of the quantum fields of matter. (Earman [2003, 565] drolly characterizes this dubious identification as "a bit of word play.") But the resulting calculation of this energy yields a value for Λ that differs from its observed value by up to 120 orders of magnitude in standard units. This has been dubbed the "cosmological constant problem" (Rugh & Zinkernagel 2002). But if it truly is a problem at all – and careful analyses cast severe doubt on it (Bianchi & Rovelli 2010, Koberinski 2021) – then it is a problem for the interpretation of the quantum field theoretic vacuum in the context of curved spacetime, rather than a problem for GR per se. It might therefore best be interpreted as a heuristic for research in quantum gravity (Schneider 2020) (although it is yet unclear how successful this has been [Koberinski 2021]).

3 Dependence and Ontology

3.1 Models as a Guide to Metaphysics

In the following subsections, I will use the structure of the models of GR as a guide to its attendant metaphysics (cf. Coffey 2014, §6). A metaphysical interpretation of GR extends the partial interpretation of Section 1, providing much more about what the theory claims beyond the broadly empirical. Roughly speaking and at a first pass, the models themselves represent possible worlds or states of affairs, while each model's *objects* and *mathematical relations* might represent its ontology and metaphysical relations (or "ideology"), respectively. Relations of functional dependence and determination between these objects and mathematical relations might represent real relations of metaphysical dependence and relative fundamentality.

This is only a "first pass" because, as we shall see in the remainder of this section, nothing *compels* one to match so neatly the formal parts of the models with what they represent. Since one can stipulate whatever "interpretational schema" one likes for a certain modeling purpose (Nguyen 2017), one cannot simply transcribe metaphysical commitments from formal structure. This would be so even if one had a recipe for transcription, for we model for many other purposes besides metaphysical clarity, such as computational efficiency, pedagogical effectiveness, or cognitive understanding (Frigg & Hartmann 2020). Also, in general, our models idealize – abstract from or distort what they represent. We can often de-idealize – augment or change a model so that it misrepresents less – but usually only in dialogue with a (perhaps temporarily) assumed interpretation.

Despite these limitations – despite being *only* a guide – the structure of the models *should* guide our interpretation of GR (*pace* Teitel 2021). An interpretation of a scientific model that harmonizes with the structure of the model facilitates surrogative reasoning with the model. This is so with metaphysical interpretations as much as it is with "concrete" ones. It is virtuous to the extent that reasoning with the model enables precision and impedes incoherence and inconsistency. With mathematical models, as we have for GR, our confidence in the consistency of the underlying mathematics underwrites, at least in part, our confidence in the consistency of the interpretation.

Interpretations of models that harmonize with the whole structure of each model are not necessary to avoid error, but it is difficult to emphasize enough how much they help given the natural tendency to interpret only certain aspects of models in isolation. A little thought experiment may illustrate this. Imagine a planet whose atmosphere is so windy that every part is in fluid motion; at each place on it, the air moves smoothly across it. Have you got it? Are you ready for metaphysical inquiry into that no windier than which can be imagined? You *haven't* and *aren't*, despite how it may seem to you. The reason is that *there can be no such planet to imagine.* The hedgehog (or "hairy ball") theorem states that there is no continuous vector field on the smooth sphere that is nowhere vanishing. If one can adequately represent the direction and magnitude of the wind on the planet with such a vector field, then its air must be still somewhere.

When the phenomena and metaphysics are complex, one can fall into incoherence without realizing how local, simple interpretations can fail to join consistently. Harmonizing interpretation with structure helps to prevent this. Still, as I alluded before in this section, neither the formal nor the nonformal aspects need to be completely fixed in the process of interpreting a theory. Given an interpretation, its ontology, properties, and (meta)physical dependencies should have formal correlates in the models. Conversely, given a set of mathematical models, their formal objects, structures, and functional dependencies should reflect the interpretations' objects, relations, and (meta)physical dependencies. Each consideration may warrant adjustment. Other virtues, besides this harmony, are relevant as well, virtues such as saving the empirical phenomena, wide scope, and economy of commitment. Thus will the structure of GR's models guide the following interpretation.

3.2 Determination and Dependence

It may seem queer to treat determination and dependence in GR, hence relative fundamentality and metaphysical dependence, before the ontology of spacetime and matter. However, queerness is virtuous for investigating the metaphysics of GR, as many of the central ontological positions and arguments turn on considerations of fundamentality and dependence. So, in this subsection, I'll first describe the facts about mathematical determination and dependence in the models of GR. Then I'll explain what interpretations these facts suggest. Next, in Section 3.3, I'll review and critically evaluate some alternative proposals for interpretations. Finally, I'll discuss determin*ism* in GR, conceptions of which will play a role in the discussion of Section 3.4.

Mathematically, within a class of models, the objects in one set, A, (nontrivially) determine simpliciter those in another, B, when those determined are a (nonconstant) function of those determining.[13] In other words, there is a

---

[13] In some cases of interest, the function may be partial, in which case one may distinguish between complete and partial determination.

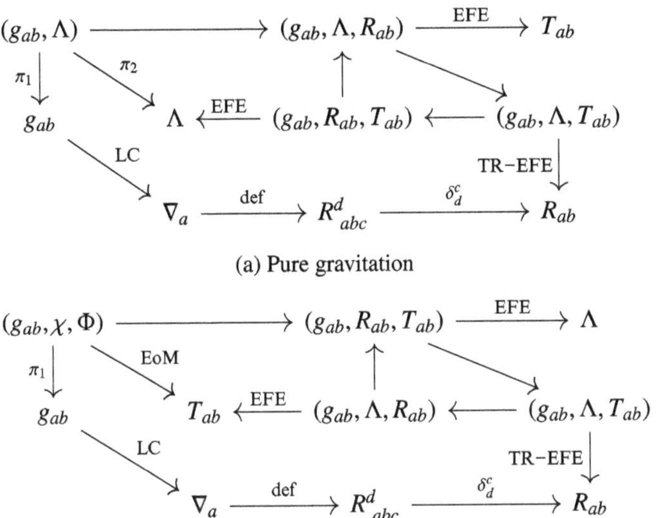

(a) Pure gravitation

(b) With matter fields and auxiliary spacetime structure

Figure 1 Commutative diagrams of the determination relations for models of GR, in the "pure" case and the case with matter and auxiliary spacetime structure. Among the objects, g_{ab} is the metric, Λ is the cosmological constant, χ is the auxiliary spacetime structure, Φ is the collection of matter fields, ∇_a is the affine connection, T_{ab} is the energy–momentum tensor, $R^d{}_{abc}$ is the Riemann tensor, and R_{ab} is the Ricci tensor. Among the arrows, π_i is the ith component projection, δ is the delta (contraction) tensor, "def" is a mathematical definition, "EoM" is the assignment of energy and momentum from the matter fields, "EFE" is the Einstein field equation, and "LC" is the Levi-Civita construction. All arrows not labeled follow from the universal property of products. (Note that the trace-reversed arrows are not needed for these.) Inessential identity and projection arrows are omitted.

(nonconstant) function $f : A \to B$ such that $f(a) = b$ if and only if the pairing (a, b) appears in one of the models. In practice, if $b \in B$ is so determined, then it is often omitted in the expression of the models, since it is specified uniquely from a. (The determining f itself rarely appears explicitly in the models.) Also in practice, B is often a space with nontrivial isomorphisms, in which case determination is only up to isomorphism: Whenever b and b' are isomorphic, the pairing (a, b) appears in the models if and only if (a, b') does. In these cases, one can still speak of functional determination, where the uniqueness of the value of the function in B for any given element in its domain A is understood to be only up to isomorphism. I will let this qualification be understood and tacit in what follows.

Figure 1 depicts the central determination relations among the objects of the models of GR, in both the cases of (a) pure gravitation and (b) matter and auxiliary spacetime structure. There are just a couple of nontrivial ones shared in both cases. First, the Levi-Civita construction, as I mentioned in Section 1, determines from the metric g_{ab} a unique, torsion-free affine connection ∇_a, hence unique associated Riemann and Ricci tensors, $R^d{}_{abc}$ and R_{ab}, respectively. Second, given the metric g_{ab}, any two from the triple $(\Lambda, R_{ab}, T_{ab})$ determines the third via the EFE and its trace-reversed version. According to the alternative I discussed in Section 2.3, in which the EFE is replaced by the trace-free EFE (Eq. (9)) and one of Eqs. (10)–(12), Λ and T_{ab} would switch places everywhere in diagram (a), making it more similar to (b), which itself would not be affected by adopting this alternative. In that case, however, (g_{ab}, χ, Φ) also determine the energy–momentum tensor T_{ab} – in principle, every component is needed. In general, none of the reverse determinations hold. (See Fletcher [2021*b*] for more details on these.) Note that the manifold M does not appear in the diagrams, as all the objects invoked (with the exception of Λ) are fields on M or (in the case of ∇_a) operators thereon.[14] So, in a way, each of them determines M (and none vice versa), but only because, considered as functions, M is their common domain.

Asymmetric determination generally suggests relative fundamentality: The more fundamental objects determine the less fundamental ones, but not vice versa. Product objects are perhaps an exception to this: They asymmetrically determine their components, but insofar as the product objects are constructed from the components, it suggests that the components are more fundamental. According to these doctrines, in any given model of either the pure gravitation or the matter cases, the metric g_{ab} of the model is more fundamental than its connection ∇_a, which is more fundamental than its Riemann tensor $R^d{}_{abc}$, which is more fundamental than its Ricci tensor R_{ab}. In both cases also the T_{ab} in the model is less fundamental than g_{ab} and Λ together, and in the nonpure gravitation case, T_{ab} is less fundamental than spacetime structure (g_{ab} and χ) and matter (Φ) together, but in general not less fundamental than either separately (cf. Lehmkuhl 2011). In no other cases is one object more fundamental than another.

Objects that (i) are not determined by any others (save for product objects) or that (perhaps also) (ii) collectively and minimally determine all other objects suggest being interpreted as the *absolutely fundamental*. These two requirements are sometimes respectively labeled as **independence** and **complete minimal basis** (Tahko 2018). We can limn fundamentalities from Figure 1: Call an object A an *ancestor* of B if there is a chain of arrows from A to B. Then objects satisfying **independence** have no ancestors themselves (save

---

[14] As I mentioned in Section 2.3, one could alternatively take Λ to be a constant scalar field on M instead of a numerical constant.

for any from product objects containing them), while a set of objects satisfying **complete minimal basis** will be a minimal ancestral set for all objects. In the pure gravitation case, g_{ab} is absolutely fundamental in the **independence** sense but not the **complete minimal basis** sense, while the converse holds for (g_{ab}, Λ). Again, according to the alternative I discussed in Section 2.3, in which the EFE is replaced by the trace-free EFE (Eq. (9)) and one of Eqs. (10)–(12), Λ would be replaced by T_{ab} in this case of pure gravitation. (The common practice of omitting Λ from the pure gravitational models usually arises not because of this alternative but because the EFE is not assumed or the value of Λ is tacitly assumed to be some fixed constant.) In the case with matter fields and auxiliary spacetime structure, each of (g_{ab}, χ, Φ) is absolutely fundamental in the **independence** sense and the collection is absolutely fundamental in the **complete minimal basis** sense.

Ehlers et al. (1972, 2012) propose a different "constructive axiomatics" for GR that also suggests different determination relations. They begin with the worldlines of free test particles and light rays as their basic objects, on which they impose conditions so that the union of these worldlines results in a Lorentzian manifold. There have been many developments and refinements of this approach; see, for example, Pfister and King (2015, Ch. 2) or Adlam et al. (2022) for recent reviews. However, a central deficiency they all share as an alternative view of the internal determination relations is that they take test matter as basic (hence seemingly absolutely fundamental) objects (cf. Sklar 1977, §VII.C). As I discuss more in Sections 3.3 and 4.1, test matter is an approximation of the matter that contributes to T_{ab} in any spacetime model representing actual phenomena. We allow it into our ontology as a convenience, if at all, justified by how it approximates more realistic matter fields. Insofar as this justification seems already to presuppose the usual spacetime structure, test matter is ill-suited to serve such a foundational role. But this does not make the this constructive program worthless. In my view, it is better to interpret it as fulfilling a role (**Examples**) analogous to that of light clocks discussed in Section 2.2 (Fletcher 2013) or to that of heuristic principles and justifications. It helps to justify why a symmetric, nondegenerate tensor field of Lorentz signature is a good representation of chronogeometric quantities, and suggests alternative theories against which GR can be tested (cf. Ehlers et al. 1972, 64).

Weaker than mathematical determination is mathematical dependence. Within a class of models consisting of tuples from a product of sets $A \times B \times \cdots$, the objects in one set, B, depend locally on A at $a \in A$ when fixing that value restricts the values of B. For example, let $S \subseteq A \times B$ be the paired objects associated with the models of interest, and suppose, without loss of generality, that dom$(S) = A$. Then B *depends locally* on A at $a \in A$ in S

when $\{b \in B : (a, b) \in S\} \neq \mathrm{ran}(S)$. *B depends locally* on A simpliciter when it depends locally on A at some $a \in A$. *B depends globally* on A when it depends locally on A for *all* $a \in A$. According to this definition, determination is a particularly strong type of global dependence in which $\{b \in B : (a, b) \in S\}$ is (up to isomorphism class) a singleton for each $a \in A$, that is, S is a function. (One can also formulate dependence in terms of multivalued functions, which can be useful for discussions of supervenience, but I leave that to another occasion.) So, all the determination relations discussed before in this subsection are also global dependence relations. But the determining tuple of objects in these cases also locally depends on the determined objects unless the determination function is constant. This dependence is global if the determination function is injective.

What are the dependence relations among the absolutely fundamental objects? Those that are absolutely fundamental in the **independence** sense can still globally depend on each other as long as that dependence doesn't rise to the level of determination. Whether matter fields Φ depend even locally on spacetime structure g_{ab}, χ or vice versa is a function of the former's equations of motion and energy–momentum contributions. (Whether χ depends on g_{ab} depends on the nature of χ. For example, time orientations will in general depend globally on g_{ab} and vice versa, but fields encoding only topological properties of M, such as its Euler characteristic, will not.) For instance, in topological field theory, there is no such mutual local dependence as M determines T_{ab}. When a matter field's contribution to energy–momentum is constant across models, as is the case with test matter, that field can well globally depend on g_{ab} without g_{ab} even locally depending on the matter field. But these tend to be exceptional cases; typically, g_{ab} and Φ depend globally on each other.

What is the *nature* of the dependence relations between all these elements? There are many options available – grounding, ontological dependence, or priority, among others (McKenzie 2022) – but much of the recent discussion has focused on whether the dependence relations between matter Φ and spacetime structure (g_{ab}, χ) are causal. For recent defenses and offenses, see respectively Weaver (2020) and Vassallo (2020), and references therein.[15] I will not intervene in this debate here except to point out that both of these authors seem to assume that Φ and g_{ab} are not mutually dependent on one another.[16] This assumption is erroneous for general matter fields if

---

¹⁵ Vassallo (2020) is primarily critical of interpreting the dependence relations as *purely* causal or grounding. He advocates instead for a mixture of the two.

¹⁶ Weaver (2020, §6.3) does offer an abductive argument for the claim that "The gravitational field's dynamical action is primary and causally prior to the inertial motion of massive bodies."

mathematical dependence guides metaphysical (or causal) dependence. Similar conclusions hold for the suggestion of Baker (2005) that Λ is a cause of motion of matter if one is considering models of GR with matter fields explicitly represented.

Whatever the interpretation of these dependence relations, it is generally acknowledged that such relations support *explanations*. In light of them, one can illuminate a challenge that Read et al. (2018, §5) pose to any interpretation of GR, namely to explain the following two coincidences (what they call "miracles"):

1. All nongravitational interactions are locally governed by Poincaré invariant dynamical laws.
2. The Poincaré symmetries of the laws governing nongravitational fields in the neighborhood of any point coincide – in the regime in which curvature can be ignored – with the symmetries of the metric field in that neighborhood.

The "invariance" and "symmetries" expressed are those of the coordinate form of the metric and the equations of motion for matter fields. This explanatory challenge is motivated by the idea that, in some sense, the symmetries of laws for matter are more fundamental than the symmetries of spacetime structure.

Strictly speaking, there is nothing to explain because the first explanandum isn't true and the second presumes the truth of the first. For example, the laws for source-free electromagnetism are invariant under a group of symmetries wider than the Poincaré symmetries, as they include conformal transformations, and the laws for the weak interaction are invariant under a smaller group of symmetries, as they must preserve orientation structure in addition to the metric. (The implications of these facts for the "dynamical" approach, discussed in Section 2.1, do not seem to have yet been fully appreciated by its proponents.)

Nonetheless, there is a line of inquiry in the conceptual vicinity without this fault: Why do the dynamical equations for matter all depend on the metric or on structures it determines? The answer is that insofar as dynamics is about change over time (or perhaps, in a generalized sense, place), it must include a representation thereof; the metric represents these times and determines the representation of change in models of GR. This is just what it means for matter dynamics to be adapted to spacetime geometry (Weatherall 2020a, §2). Matter dynamics depends only on the spacetime structure there is, while whatever spacetime structure there is depends on (because it must include) whatever

---

In any case, even for readers who follow his argument, whether one dependency is "primary" or "prior" isn't apparently relevant to the fact of mutual dependence at hand.

structure the matter dynamics presupposes. Neither is more fundamental than the other, in line with the conclusions drawn previously in this subsection.

The line of inquiry might continue: Isn't it a coincidence that all matter fields involve the same notions of time, distance, and change? Couldn't there be notions of these bespoke to particular types of matter? I can think of three sorts of answers to this second question. The first is dismissive:

1. Is this a coincidence worth an explanation? What was one expecting, after all? If this is a coincidence, it is not unique to GR, but applies equally to all spacetime theories, relativistic and nonrelativistic. It has been an adequate modeling assumption for all of these, and there is no clear evidence otherwise. That's why Newton, in the Scholium to his *Principia*, makes this same assumption.

One can also well resist on conceptual grounds that this is a coincidence, or that it cannot be explained through a kind of theoretical equivalence. The second and third answers elaborate on this pair of conceptual responses in particular ways.

2. If in fact there is only one matter field, only one representation of time, length, and change is needed. Such a unified field theory needn't have the strong ambitions of grand unified theories in particle physics to have a simple Lie group as the gauge group for matter; allowing product gauge groups would suffice as long as one could interpret values in this space as that of a single material field. One could argue that this has already been achieved in the Standard Model of particle physics.
3. Suppose that there were matter fields with separate notions of time, distance, and change, and yet those fields interacted. If it is possible to rewrite their dynamical equations in terms of a single metric (or metric-like) structure – representing just one notion of time, distance, and change, perhaps with extra spacetime structure – then such a theory with, for example, multiple structures representing time would be equivalent with one with a single such structure. Some such theories have already been proposed, especially in the context of problems in cosmology (e.g., Hossenfelder 2008, Hohmann 2014, Petit & d'Agostini 2014). Brans-Dicke theory (Weinstein 1996) and TeVeS (Brown 2005, §9.5.2) may also count as examples.[17]

These sketches of answers deserve fuller pursuit than I can sustain here. It is worth emphasizing nonetheless that the questions to which they respond do

---

[17] See also Lucas (1973) for an earlier philosophical discussion of the possibility of more than one temporal structure.

not concern the interpretation of GR per se. Just as one can stipulate what the metric represents, one need give no apology for a single metric (and associated structure) if it appears to be representationally adequate. The explanations that these questions entreat draw not from a single theory, but an implicit collection of alternatives, responding to how one might account for some atypicality of GR within this class (Weatherall 2011, Lehmkuhl et al. 2016).

3.3 Ontology of Gravity and of Spacetime Structure

The traditional ontological debate in the philosophy of space is between positions we now call *substantivalism* and *relationalism* (Pooley 2013). Substantivalists maintain that space is a sort of entity that exists independently of matter, while relationalists insist that space is only an abstraction from the spatial relations between material bodies or parts thereof. In the transition to modern and relativistic physics, an analogous debate continues concerning spacetime, hence concerning the status of spatiotemporal structures.

Before addressing this debate and how the interpretation of Section 1 interfaces with it, I will discuss the distinction between and identification of spacetime structure and matter. This distinction raises issues about the interpretation of test matter. I then draw some consequences for the ontology of gravity itself and its relation to the notion of a gravitational field in GR. Only then do I return to the initial question about the ontology of spacetime, with the results of the previous discussion in hand.

As I mentioned in Section 1, the interpretation of GR I described there has two sorts: spacetime structure and matter fields. For each of these sorts, I mentioned a representational criterion and a formal criterion, which (with one exception to be explained presently) align as necessary and sufficient conditions that partition the fields into the two sorts. Matter fields are the stuff that events are (at least potentially) about: They involve coincidence values of these fields. Familiar cases, such as the density and pressure of fluids and the strength of electromagnetic fields, illustrate this, but it can be difficult to apply to unfamiliar cases. The formal criterion is much easier to apply: Matter fields are just those fields for which there is an explicit procedure for how they variably contribute to the energy–momentum, in the sense that the latter is a function of (hence, determined by) the values of the former. That matter fields interact means that they have the potential to exchange energy and momentum, leading to differences in their dynamics.

Test matter presents a problem case for the alignment of these criteria: It ostensibly represents stuff that events could be about, but it does not contribute to energy–momentum. One response to this is to interpret the criteria as not logical criteria but cluster criteria, in the sense that something is more deserving of the title "matter" to the extent that it satisfies each of the criteria (Baker 2021). Test matter then occupies a liminal position between (nontest) matter and spacetime structure because it satisfies enough, but not too many, of the cluster criteria for both. However, I prefer instead of adopting cluster criteria to make an explicit exception for test matter in light of its theoretical role in GR and in spacetime theory more generally. We allow for test matter in our models to the extent that it approximates, as a limiting case, the properties of matter fields that do contribute to energy–momentum. This will present a contrast with spacetime structure. (Although I favor this sort of interpretation of test matter, in Section 4.1, I will discuss in more detail one other way of how to implement this interpretation of test matter by reviving the old distinction between active and passive charges or properties.)

Unlike matter, spacetime structure is not stuff that events are about, but rather encodes spatiotemporal properties of collections of events. In other words, spacetime structure represents spatiotemporal concepts. In GR, these include the familiar cases of duration, length, angle, change, and so on, as represented by the metric g_{ab} and possibly an orientation field. Like with the representational criterion for matter, this may be difficult to apply when faced with an unfamiliar structure, and there is some vagueness regarding which concepts are spatiotemporal. Also as before, the formal criterion is much easier to apply: Fields that represent spatiotemporal structure are just those that do not contribute variably to the energy–momentum. Test matter fields are an explicit exception; spacetime structure is not generally the limit of (nontest) matter.

Discussions of spacetime structure often have *various* spacetime theories as their subject. Although such generalization is not my primary object here, I would venture that the formal criterion of energy–momentum contribution would be the most important when exploring the interpretation of an unfamiliar proposal for a spacetime theory. If such a theory is not explicitly stipulated to represent spatiotemporal concepts, as some claim to be the case with certain models of quantum gravity, then "spacetime structure" might be a misnomer, even if the contrast with matter is still apt. It may in such theories be the case that the candidates one identifies for representing emergent spacetime are partly "pre-spatiotemporal" and partly material.

In any case, this generalization, focusing on the formal criterion, also contrasts with other recent characterizations of matter and spacetime structure in the literature, of which I'll consider three. First, Martens and Lehmkuhl (2020) present a list of eight criteria of increasing strength for matter and eight criteria for spacetime structure. However, both sets of criteria are unsatisfactory. Their weakest matter criterion is that "The object under consideration is not constant/static, but varies/changes." Static, nonvacuum relativistic spacetimes fail this criterion but by stipulation contain matter fields, such as perfect fluids. Unless one wants to eliminate such models as physical possibilities, this and all their other criteria cannot be necessary. Their spacetime structure criteria just stipulate that particular structures, such as Lorentzian manifolds or affine connections, represent spacetime structure, but no mathematical structure represents anything spatiotemporal in virtue of its mathematical properties alone.

Second, Baker (2021, S290) proposes that spacetime structure is a cluster concept, listing nine different criteria (without claiming completeness). One criterion is my formal criterion, that spacetime structure does not carry energy or momentum. While I'm sympathetic to the idea that many natural concepts are cluster concepts, I'm also not convinced that any of the other criteria he listed have much independent weight. Many of them, like the criteria of Martens and Lehmkuhl (2020), are much too specific to particular mathematical structures, or are plausible only to the extent that they presuppose the functional, representational criterion, such as "ground[ing] or explain[ing] a family of modal facts about which states are *geometrically* possible."

Third, Knox (2019, 122) proposes a functionalist criterion just for spacetime structure: "spacetime is whatever serves to define a structure of inertial frames, where inertial frames are those in whose coordinates the laws governing interactions take a simple form (that is universal insofar as curvature may be ignored), and with respect to which free bodies move with constant velocity."

The representational component of my criterion also has a functionalist flavor, but locates the function more broadly in spatiotemporal concepts rather than narrowly in inertial frames. (Read and Menon [2021, §5] note this alternative functionalist possibility but rightly complain that it makes it difficult to apply to unfamiliar cases, as I acknowledge. The formal component of my criterion, I should emphasize by contrast, is not functionalist.) This narrower conception leads to unsatisfactory results even just within GR (even setting aside what it means for the laws to be "simple"). In one respect, it is too narrow: It rules out orientation structure, since orientation plays no role in determining inertial frames. It also rules out the spacetime metric, since neither the signature of the metric nor its scale factor are needed to determine such inertial frames: The metric provides more structure than is needed. If one generously allows any formal structure that provides at least enough to define inertial frames to count as spacetime structure, then any contrived amalgam with at least this much will count. In another respect, it is too broad: In perfect fluid models, the velocity vector field of the fluid defines a frame in which the equations of motion simplify even further (Fletcher 2020*a*), but this field represents material, not spacetime structure. If one generously allows any structure representing material structure that provides at least enough to define inertial frames to count as spacetime structure, then too much material structure will also count as spacetime structure. (See Baker [2021] and Read and Menon [2021] for further criticisms.)

Turning now to the ontology of the gravity itself, Lehmkuhl (2008) provides a helpful classification of three types of positions concerning the relative ontological priority of gravity and spacetime geometry.

Geometric Gravitation reduces to, or is nothing more than, a manifestation of spacetime geometry.

Field Spacetime geometry reduces to, or is nothing more than, a manifestation of gravitation, that is, the gravitational field.

Egalitarian Gravitation and spacetime geometry are identical, with neither reducing to the other.

Spacetime geometry consists of the facts about durations, lengths, angles, changes, and so on that the metric represents. "Gravitation" is more imprecise: It refers to the more vaguely defined class of gravitational phenomena whose common source one might reify in a material gravitational *field*. Lehmkuhl (2008, §4) considers three candidates for such a reification, including the connection components (Einstein's preference), opting for the metric itself, since it determines all the other objects that have gravitational significance – that is, those that play a role in describing gravitational phenomena. One can see this in Figure 1(a) (taking a tacit, fixed value of the cosmological constant).

However, the fact that the metric determines the other structures of a relativistic spacetime with gravitational significance does not entail that it represents a material gravitational field or potential. There are also two positive reasons against it. First, the usual conception of a field or potential, from matter theory, is that there is a zero section of the field bundle that represents a vanishing field, the absence of the field's material effects. In the case of gravitation, one should find this at least in Minkowski spacetime, which characteristically represents a relativistic universe (or a portion of one) in the absence of gravitation. But the metric, always being nondegenerate, admits of no zero section. It does not help to identify the gravitational field as the difference between the metric g_{ab} and the Minkowski metric η_{ab} (cf. Pooley 2013, 539n34), for this quantity is not well defined when the underlying manifold is *not* $\mathbb{R}^4$, and not uniquely defined when the underlying manifold *is* $\mathbb{R}^4$ (Fletcher & Weatherall 2023*a*).

This suggests a better candidate to represent the source of gravitational effects: Lehmkuhl's other candidate, the Riemann tensor $R^a{}_{bcd}$ (Synge 1960, viii). It vanishes in Minkowski spacetime and in all and only other spacetimes where, by definition, there is no spacetime curvature. Lehmkuhl (2008, 96) objects that this does not allow one to describe a "homogeneous" gravitational field, even in idealization, but the basis of the objection seems to be incorrect. Insofar as a homogeneous gravitational field is an object of Newtonian gravitation, it can be expressed as the limit, or idealization, of certain general relativistic models (Fletcher 2019).

That said, even if the Riemann tensor encodes the local phenomena of gravitation, it cannot be interpreted as a *material* field according to my criteria for matter fields. This is because it does not contribute to energy–momentum. The same applies to the metric itself. Moreover, the phenomena of gravitation is not *merely* local; it may manifest across quite extended collections of events without appreciable curvature.

Although I postpone further discussion of gravitational energy to Section 4.3, I can note here that this second reason against interpreting the metric in particular as a material field bears upon some suggestions that it must be material because it obeys its "own" dynamical equations, the EFE, and that it acts on and reacts against matter fields (Brown 2005). Rovelli (1997, 197) expresses the idea forcefully:

> A strong burst of gravitational waves could come from the sky and knock down the rock of Gibraltar, precisely as a strong burst of electromagnetic radiation could. Why is the first "matter" and the second "space"? Why should we regard the second burst as ontologically different from the second? Clearly the distinction can now be seen as ill-founded.

If the EFE is really a dynamical equation for the metric, it must express how the metric changes from one event to another. But according to what standard is the metric changing? The only absolute standard available for change – that is, one not relative to some auxiliary structure – is the derivative operator ∇_a, but its compatibility condition ensures that $\nabla_a g_{bc} = \mathbf{0}$, that is, the metric is *unchanging* within a model. This is because the derivative operator just extends the notion of change that the metric itself provides. The metric cannot be dynamical merely because the metric is not a fixed field, as is the case in special relativity or Newtonian spacetime, because auxiliary spacetime structure, such as orientation fields, are not fixed but are clearly nonmaterial. In any case, there is no logical implication from being dynamical to being material: The British monarchy, for instance, obeys its own peculiar dynamical rules of succession, but not even the staunchest royalists consider it thereby a material entity.

The rhetoric of action and reaction here is also unclear. It is true that, as discussed in the previous subsection, the metric and matter typically depend upon one another. But this dependence, however it is interpreted, need not entail material interaction, just as the dependence between any sort of properties across events need not, as the example of the monarchy just discussed attests.

It is also true that the metric typically appears in the equations of motion for material fields, but that is not sufficient to conclude that they interact, as any such equations invoking auxiliary spacetime structure, such as an orientation, attest. Moreover, material fields "act" on each other typically in virtue of energy–momentum exchange or conversion as represented by contributions to T_{ab}, but the metric has no such energy to give, or so I will argue in Sections 4.3–4.4, even for gravitational waves. (In those sections, I will consider attributing to the metric a kind of energy relative to a frame field that defines a local flat metric, but that relative energy is not the sort invoked in the criterion for material interaction, as the local flat metric can be chosen conventionally and independently of the behavior of matter.)

I conclude against gravitation requiring – really, *permitting* – a separate material entity, a gravitational field, which rules out both **Field** and **Egalitarian**, the latter because it requires postulating a material gravitational field in addition to (or identical with) spacetime geometry. The spacetime metric and the structures it determines just do not have the necessary properties to be regarded as material fields. Still, I emphasize that the "spacetime geometry" in **Geometric** is just a codification of the structure of durations, lengths, and so on – gravitation reduces to, or is nothing more than that.

Finally, I return to the question with which I started this subsection: Does spacetime and its structure exist independently from material things (substantivalism) or are spacetime and its structure just abstractions of or derivative from relations between material things, and perhaps their parts (relationalism)? I have established twofold criteria for material fields and spacetime structure and argued that the two are disjoint in GR: g_{ab} and χ (and perhaps Λ) represent spacetime structure, while Φ represents material fields. So one can answer the question by considering whether GR permits spacetime events (or whole spacetimes more generally) with only spacetime structure and no material things. Pure gravitational models and those whose material fields all vanish at some event are therefore those that the relationalist must extirpate from the theory or explain away. Extirpation is costly, for these models play important (and not clearly eliminable) explanatory roles in the application of GR. There is a general strategy for explaining away, however: Affirm that the spacetime models in question are merely *abstractions* from models with nonvanishing matter fields (perhaps including test matter) at every event. In this case, events still represent the partlike coincidences of material things, but some of those things might not be represented in the spacetime model. The cost of relationalism without culling some of the models of GR is therefore the theory's representational incompleteness.

Subtanativalists pay a different cost for these models. They do not need to hold that they are representationally incomplete, but to do so they must slightly change the interpretation of events themselves. In light of the models in question, events cannot in general be the *actual* partlike coincidences of material fields; they are rather the *possible* such coincidences. The cost of substantivalism is therefore introducing an intrinsically modal interpretation of some of the basic posits of GR. Perhaps one way of reducing that cost is a variant of substantivalism called *super*substantivalism. In the context of GR, this position maintains that matter fields are in fact properties of spacetime events rather than things (substances) with independent existence (Lehmkuhl 2018). This suggests interpreting the mathematical points of spacetime not as events at all, but as a *sui generis* substance of hyperregions that may or may not have nonvanishing material field strengths. The cost that this version pays in exchange for the modality of events is a more unfamiliar basic ontology.

3.4 Determinism and the Hole Argument

In the previous subsection, I did not uphold either relationalism or (super) substantivalism: Each has its own costs and benefits and is tenable given the other interpretative commitments I do uphold. But there is an argument, the (so-called) "hole argument," which purports to expose a hidden cost of any substantival interpretation. The argument asks us to consider two isometric relativistic spacetimes, (M, g, Λ) and $(M, \tilde{g}, \Lambda)$, such that the diffeomorphism $\psi : M \rightarrow M$ giving rise to the witnessing isometry is the identity exactly outside of an open set (the "hole") $O \subset M$ with compact closure. A proponent of substantivalism (the argument continues) must maintain that (M, g, Λ) and $(M, \tilde{g}, \Lambda)$ represent distinct spacetimes because in general they assign different metrical values to points $p \in O$. Yet the laws of GR do not uniquely determine whether (M, g, Λ) or $(M, \tilde{g}, \Lambda)$ develops from any proper initial data hypersurface outside of O, if there is one. Thus, the argument concludes, the substantivalist is committed to an untoward and pernicious form of indeterminism. It is untoward in the face of a norm that physics, not metaphysics, should decide substantive questions of determinism; it is pernicious because it applies to all local properties in O.

As John Stachel first discussed in 1980, the contours of the hole argument originate with Einstein's labors to find the EFE. Earman and Norton (1987) then redrew those contours towards the ontological conclusion against substantivalism. The vast majority of attempts to defuse the argument employ some metaphysical maneuvering in reformulating substantivalism or determinism. (The scholarly literature on the hole argument is now too enormous to canvas here, but see Norton et al. [2023] and Pooley [2021] for further introduction and references.) By contrast, following the general argumentative strategy of Weatherall (2018), in this subsection I will elaborate why one can defuse the argument by considering only the *representational* principles of GR. (The argument I give is different in particulars from the one in Weatherall [2018]; I comment on some of those differences in my responses to skeptics of representational responses later in this subsection.)

Before I do so, consider the notion of *determinism* invoked in the hole argument. It is a version of Laplacian determinism (Hoefer 2016), the rough idea of which is that for any time and state of the universe at that time, there is a unique way the universe could be for all times: Any instantaneous state determines all. This is what the initial data hypersurface and the question of a unique spacetime development in the argument refer to.

However it's made precise, determinism for a theory is a doctrine about certain determination relations, much in the sense of those discussed in Section 3.2, but with two important differences (cf. Butterfield 1989, Doboszewski 2019). First, they have different relata. Instead of, for instance, the (global) metric determining the (global) affine connection, one considers certain fields on, for instance, an achronal region of spacetime determining certain fields on the rest of spacetime. This is significant for GR because the relevant analogue of a "state at a time" may not exist for all general relativistic models. Consequently one can adopt a determinism "schema" with the relevant region, structure thereon, and structure determined thereby as open variables. In the case of the hole argument, one can then take advantage of the fact that every point of every spacetime has a neighborhood which, considered as a spacetime in its own right, is globally hyperbolic. For various standard matter fields, including electromagnetic fields and many perfect fluids, every initial dataset for this neighborhood has a (maximal) development in this neighborhood, unique up to isomorphism (Hawking & Ellis 1973, Ch. 7.7), in which one can select O to lie.

This uniqueness *only up to isomorphism* is the second difference that determinism's notion of determination demands. There is a conceptual reason for this that finds widespread implementation in practice. That reason is that the question of determinism is only interesting regarding properties that a theory represents, which are those invariant under the isomorphisms of the theory's models. Otherwise, even the simplest theories fail to be deterministic. For instance, the usual dynamics of balls rolling down ramps would be radically indeterministic because the initial conditions don't determine the color of the ball at any other time. In the case of GR, no property or structure variant under isometry is represented. One sees this in practice among general relativists, for example, in work on the initial value problem and in debates about the Cosmic Censorship Hypothesis, the claim (roughly) that globally hyperbolic spacetimes are generic among the "physically reasonable" spacetimes, the ones that represent genuine physical possibilities. (See, e.g., Smeenk and Wüthrich [2021] for a recent review.) The significance of this is that if there are properties of the target of the spacetime models not represented in the models and not determined by an initial data surface, then the sort of indeterminism involved, such as it would be, is not at all untoward (cf. Norton 2020, Weatherall 2020*b*, §3).

The chestnut at the heart of these observations, that scientific models (including those of GR) are often abstracted, is also the core insight assuaging certain problem examples for the foregoing understanding of determinism. These examples involve an indeterministic symmetry-breaking process, such as a beam buckling to one side or other, radioactive decay products emanating at some angle or other, or a particle swerving in one direction or another (e.g., Belot 1995, Melia 1999). One would like to say that there is more than one direction in which the process could have happened, yet all the models that represent these processes are putatively isomorphic, hence would count them as deterministic. But if one does not represent the different directions explicitly in the model, such as with an orientation field, it is no surprise that the models give unwelcome answers to questions pertaining to those directions, just as the question of the color of a rolling ball did above in classical mechanics. Using models to reason about properties they don't represent can easily drive one into error. But once one adds a representation of these properties, say through an orientation field, the models are no longer isomorphic: Some processes go in one direction, others in another. (See Fletcher [2020*b*] for further elaboration on representational capacities, especially in the context of the hole argument.)

Now return to the hole argument. It highlights a formal property, $g_{|p}$, of a spacetime model that is variant across isometric spacetimes: $g_{|p} \neq \tilde{g}_{|p} = \psi_*(g)_{|p}$. However, the very fact that this property is variant across isometric spacetimes shows that spacetime models cannot represent anything with it – it is not even *implicitly definable* in the models of the theory. So, either really there is no physical property to represent – just as no number-theoretic property is represented by the particular construction of the integers in set theory – or there is such a property, which has been abstracted from the models. In the former case, there are no undetermined properties. In the latter case, this entails not an untoward but a totally benign sort of indeterminism, as the foregoing discussion established.

One could, of course, augment the model by adding auxiliary spacetime structure – say, a distinguished point p or open region O of the manifold – to represent properties assigned to the hole. But in this case determinism still holds, for then by construction ψ witnesses that $(\psi(M), \psi_*(g), \Lambda, \psi(O)) = (M, \tilde{g}, \Lambda, \psi(O))$ is isomorphic to (M, g, Λ, O). ψ provides a kind of "counterpart" relation, a means to compare the structures and properties that the two spacetime models represent, and according to it they represent the same properties. Relative to other maps implementing such a relation, such as the identity $1_M : M \rightarrow M$, the models therefore represent different properties. There is no ambiguity about what each model represents together once one specifies the map relative to which they are compared.

There have been several objections to representational responses to the hole argument. Landsman (2022, §§1.10, 7.8) appears to focus on seeming controversies about the sense in which ψ and 1_M are counterpart relations, asserting that one avoids invoking them and "reopens" the hole argument by reformulating the scenario to which it appeals in terms of the initial value problem. However, that I also formulated it in this way in my own representational response shows that the focus on these maps as essential to the core representational response is a red herring. Pooley (2021, 154) insists that without metaphysical commitments, the representational response does not succeed in blocking the hole argument: "[I]f there are pluralities of merely haecceististically distinct possibilities, the mathematical formalism of GR, correctly interpreted, is necessarily indifferent to differences between them.... And that, of course, is just to admit that, according to any metaphysical view committed to such pluralities, GR is indeterministic." But as I emphasized earlier in this subsection, this is a *benign* indeterminism because it involves properties not represented at all in the models. My statement of its harmlessness is not a metaphysical thesis but one about how scientific models represent. Moreover, the representational response is agnostic on the existence of these possibilities because they arise only in the conditional reasoning of one branch of the response's constructive dilemma.

Roberts (2020, 255) objects that some pairs of isometric Lorentzian manifolds "cannot be concretely interpreted to represent the same physical situation at once" as would be required by the general doctrine, employed in the representational response, that isomorphic models $(M, \tilde{g}, \Lambda)$ and (M, g, Λ) could represent one and the same state of affairs. The example he uses is a two-dimensional half-plane $M = \mathbb{R} \times (0, \infty)$ with the Minkowski metric restricted to it, and submanifold $\tilde{M} = \mathbb{R} \times (s, \infty)$, with $s > 0$, also with the Minkowski metric restricted to it. These two models, (M, g) and $(\tilde{M}, \tilde{g})$, are isometric, but because $\tilde{M} \subset M$, "one cannot use them both to represent the same thing at once, on pain of paradoxes of multiple denotation" (Roberts 2020, 263). What are these paradoxes? Roberts illustrates with an informal example: It is a convention whether we label one side of Manhattan "East" and the other

"West." Consequently, using maps with each convention together would permit one to assert that "The New York Public Library is located on the East side and on the West side (not on the East side)" (Roberts 2020, 252).

As this example illustrates, however, seeming contradiction arises only by leaving tacit how each cardinal direction ascription is relative to a particular convention. Once those conventions are made explicit again – for example, "The New York Public Library is located on the East$_1$ side and on the West$_2$ side" – no contradiction arises. In practice, these conventions are shared or context provides enough information about which is intended, as is generically the case with indexical words. The same moral applies to GR: In the example of Roberts, relative to the identity inclusion $i : \tilde{M} \rightarrow M$, $(\tilde{M}, \tilde{g})$ represents a proper part of (M, g) and the two would not represent the same state of affairs; indeed, i is not even a diffeomorphism. But relative to the diffeomorphism $\psi_s : M \rightarrow \tilde{M}$, they can well represent the same state of affairs at once. Once again, there is no ambiguity about what each model represents together once one specifies the map relative to which they are compared. In a word, there are no relevant paradoxes of multiple denotation, either in natural language or in GR.

4 Energy

4.1 The Functions of Energy–Momentum and the Nature of Test Matter

Energy and momentum have several functions in GR. One is to constrain spacetime curvature via the EFE (Eq. (1)). Considering this equation as a partial differential equation in which manifold points are the independent variable and spacetime metrics are the dependent variable, energy and momentum act as a *source* for gravitational phenomena (solutions to the equation). But, as discussed in Section 3.2, one should not infer that this technical notion of "source" is that of a cause without acknowledging the substantive additional interpretational commitment this incurs.

Another function of energy and momentum, common to field and mechanical theories, is to aid in the description and explanation of matter dynamics. For instance, given a Lagrangian density for a matter theory, its energy–momentum tensor T^{ab} is defined by an algebraic combination of the Lagrangian, its derivatives and independent variables, and the spacetime metric (Hawking & Ellis 1973, Ch. 3.3, Wald 1984, Ch. E.1). In fact, the field equations arising as the Euler–Lagrange equations for the matter fields alone then guarantee that the total energy–momentum so defined will be divergence-free, that is, satisfy **conservation** $\nabla_a T^{ab} = 0$ (Hawking & Ellis 1973, 67,

Weatherall 2019, §3).[18] (There is some controversy about whether "$\nabla_a T^{ab} = \mathbf{0}$" really expresses a conservation law, which I address in Section 4.2.) But even if the matter theory's dynamics are not given by a Lagrangian, energy and momentum assignments facilitate the dynamical analysis of material behavior, often through conservation laws. **Conservation** is so important to the function of energy and momentum in the analysis of physical theories that Hawking and Ellis (1973, 61) *require* that any adequate matter theory must assign energy–momentum so that $\nabla_a T^{ab} = \mathbf{0}$.

Notably, in GR, the *same* tensor field performs both functions: T^{ab} is both the source in the EFE *and* facilitates the description and explanation of matter dynamics, especially through its conservation. This substantial functional unification is part of the sense in which GR explains the coincidence, in Newtonian gravitation, of the proportionality of inertial and gravitational mass: There is only one (fundamental) mass concept, the inertial mass, which is a component of or contributes to energy and momentum (Weatherall 2011).

Aside from **conservation**, so-called *energy conditions* constitute another class of constraints commonly imposed on adequate matter theories, although enthusiasm for them has dwindled over the decades (Barcelo & Visser 2002). Such conditions are inequalities concerning T_{ab} in relation to ideal observers or reference frames – see Curiel (2017) for a comprehensive review. For instance, I mentioned the **DEC** in Section 2.2, which holds at an event when the flux density of energy–momentum at that event be the sort that one could associate with a massive test particle or light ray (according to **Histories** and **Light**). In Section 5.2, I discuss how notions of relativistic causality – how, if at all, events in spacetime affect one another – implicates **DEC**.

Another kind of constraint on adequate matter theories concerns exclusively the energetic effects of vanishing fields. Hawking and Ellis (1973, 61–62) propose that "T^{ab} vanishes on an open set $\mathcal{U}$ [of M] if and only if all the matter fields vanish on $\mathcal{U}$," which "expresses the principle that all fields have energy." Clearly this requirement assumes that matter fields can "vanish," that is, they are values in a bundle that has a "zero" section. Hawking and Ellis (1973, 62) also acknowledge that one might object to the "only if" direction of the biconditional with the example of two matter fields whose contributions to T_{ab} cancel each other exactly on $\mathcal{U}$. Reformulating the constraint on a field-by-field basis alleviates this problem:

---

[18] Noether's first theorem guarantees a conservation law for the "canonical" energy–momentum if the Lagrangian is invariant under the flow induced by the subgroup of translations of the Poincaré group, but the canonical energy–momentum is not always the same as that defined through the Lagrangian directly (Wald 1984, 456–459). See, e.g., Baker et al. (2022) for a discussion of this issue.

All Fields Have Energy (AFHE) For any matter field ϕ, its contribution to T^{ab} vanishes on an open set $\mathcal{U} \subseteq M$ if and only if ϕ vanishes on $\mathcal{U}$.

At least in the case of Lagrangian theories, one can make the notion of "contribution" more precise and even prove **AFHE**, subject to the assumption that the Lagrangian density for a field (and its interactions) vanishes only when the field vanishes (Weatherall 2019, §3).

There are, however, still two complications for **AFHE**. One arises for quantum fields. For these, a "zero section" most plausibly refers to a ground state. Although the most general frameworks for quantum theory do not require such a state, it is a typical and well-motivated enough assumption. More problematically, ground states commonly have nonvanishing contributions to energy, which challenges the "if" direction of **AFHE**. That said, this energy is typically proportional to some power of Planck's constant h, meaning that its classical limit is plausibly zero. In these cases, **AFHE** might still hold of matter fields that can be treated classically.

The other complication arises for test matter. As I discussed in Sections 1 and 2.2, test matter – including test particles – is matter whose dynamics depends on the metric and the notion of change it determines, but which does not contribute to the energy–momentum that sources the EFE. There is no question of test matter conflicting with any of the energy conditions, but it does violate the "only if" part of **AFHE**. I see at least four mutually exclusive options one can take with respect to this conflict.

1. Decline to attribute energy and momentum to test matter.

However, in practice, one does ineliminably refer to and describe the energy and momentum of test particles and fields to facilitate the description and explanation of its dynamics, which is inconsistent with this option's understanding of test matter.

2. Decline the "only if" part of **AFHE**.

This option weakens **AFHE** by assuming that test matter *does* contribute to T_{ab}. In other words, it gives up on there being any distinction between test matter and ordinary matter. It's possible to restore this division by introducing an old distinction sometimes found in discussions of mass in Newtonian gravitation.

3. Subdivide energy–momentum into two types, *active* and *passive*, and restrict **AFHE** to active energy–momentum. Test matter then is a sort of matter with vanishing active energy–momentum; its passive energy–momentum is just that invoked in relation to its dynamics.

Passive energy–momentum plays an inertial role and helps describe how matter is affected by gravitational phenomena, while active energy–momentum describes how matter affects gravitational phenomena (through the EFE).

In its disunification of energy–momentum, this option thus contravenes the conclusion I had drawn earlier in this subsection, that the same tensor field performs both functions for energy–momentum (a source in the EFE and its role in describing and explaining dynamics). By the same token, it also raises difficult questions about what, exactly, test matter represents according to this option. There are no known matter fields – real test fields – for which active and passive energy–momentum would truly differ.[19] Rather, one introduces test fields only to model matter whose sourcing effects are negligible relative to a modeling purpose.

For these reasons, over these first three options, I prefer a fourth:[20]

4. Deny that test matter is a type of matter field at all. Instead, affirm that the "test" attribute denotes that one is *approximating* a matter field's source contribution to the EFE as zero.

This options relies on a distinction between idealizations and approximations inspired by that of Norton (2012). For present purposes, an idealization is a model of GR that is less representationally accurate than another, while an approximation is a property attribution (e.g., to a matter field) that is less representationally accurate than another. The property attributions in approximations need not be possible according to the models of GR; they are therefore introduced only for pragmatic convenience.

The third option would therefore take GR models with test fields to be idealizations of GR models with nontest fields replacing the test fields. The present, fourth option rather does not admit test fields as components of models of GR, but as denoting an approximation of the intended field's energy–momentum. The worldlines of test *particles*, accordingly, are themselves approximations of highly localized field distributions. (Indeed, as I will discuss in more detail in Section 5.2, this option also coheres best with work on the relation between energy conditions and relativistic causality.) This solves the problems of compatibility with applications that the previous options had. It also retains a functionally unified account of energy–momentum, is compatible with **AFHE**, and explains further why I take **Histories**, **Freedom**, and **Light** not to be fundamental representational principles of GR – they concern the interpretation of mere approximations. The cost of this option is acknowledging that the inferences one makes in using the

---

[19] More precisely, if they do differ, their difference is by a constant of proportionality that can be conventionally set to one.

[20] Another problem with options 2 and 3 is that they would also seem to require representing pointlike test matter with distributions; see Weatherall (2020*a*, §2.1) for some of the delicate mathematical issues with this.

test matter approximation may be fallible to the degree that the approximation is substantial, and accepting the responsibility to confirm, when necessary, that the error incurred is not too large.

4.2 Conservation of Energy–Momentum

In the previous section, I asserted that "$\nabla_a T^{ab} = 0$" expresses a conservation law for the energy–momentum T^{ab}. On the one hand, this is common enough in physics-oriented presentations that it rarely engenders further comment or justification. On the other hand, some authors deny it, many even going so far as to reject that energy–momentum is generally conserved at all in GR (Hoefer 2000, Lam 2011, Dürr 2019). Although they give various reasons for this, the central one is that Eq. (10) ("$\nabla_a T^{ab} = 0$") "cannot be used to write an integral conservation law . . . .. Intuitively, if energy–momentum is *really* being conserved locally, then when one integrates [it] up it should be conserved over regions as well" (Hoefer 2000, 191).

This objection refers to the following procedure. As discussed in connection with the **DEC**, for any $p \in M$ and any unit timelike $\xi^a \in T_p M$, $T^{ab}\xi_b$ represents the energy–momentum flux density at p relative to a frame at p with timelike component ξ^a. If one extends ξ^a to a C^1 timelike vector field on an oriented hypersurface $S \subset M$, then one can integrate $T^{ab}\xi_b$ over S to calculate the net energy–momentum flux through that surface: $\int_S T^{ab}\xi_b d_a\sigma$, where σ is the (oriented) volume form on M. (The sign of the orientation merely determines the sign of the flux.) In particular, if S is the boundary of a precompact n-dimensional submanifold $\mathcal{U}$ and one extends ξ^a to $\mathcal{U}$, then by Gauss's theorem,

$$\int_S T^{ab}\xi_b d_a\sigma = \int_{\mathcal{U}} \nabla_a(T^{ab}\xi_b)\sigma. \tag{14}$$

This states that the net energy–momentum flux through S is equal to the integral of the energy–momentum *source density* $\nabla_a(T^{ab}\xi_b)$ over $\mathcal{U}$. (So, *pace* Hoefer [2000], it is not the energy–momentum itself that one integrates – after all, T^{ab} is a two-index tensor field for which in general direct integration is not well-defined – but either its flux, through a hypersurface, or its source density, over a compact four-dimensional region.[21]) Conservation holds if either side of Eq. (14) vanishes for all choices of $\mathcal{U}$ and any suitable choice of ξ^a.

But what makes a choice of ξ^a suitable? Not just any is. It is well-known that choosing ξ^a as a field with nonvanishing acceleration prevents these integrals

---

[21] Lam (2011, 1016) also misleadingly describes expressions like the left-hand side of Eq. (14) as "the quantity of nongravitational energy in a spatial (three-dimensional) region" rather than the net flux through that region.

from vanishing – even in mundane, classical mechanical cases – because such fields can only well represent frames that generate noninertial coordinate systems, whose fictitious forces can appear to do work on a system whose energy–momentum are clearly conserved (Duerr 2019, 4). Lam (2011) and Dürr (2019) suggest that the only suitable ξ^a is a timelike Killing vector field (KVF), that is, one that satisfies Killing's equation, $\nabla_{(a}\xi_{b)} = \mathbf{0}$.[22] For in this case, the source density vanishes: $\nabla_a(T^{ab}\xi_b) = (\nabla_a T^{ab})\xi_b + T^{ab}(\nabla_a\xi_b)$, where the first term vanishes because of Eq. (10) and the second term vanishes because of Killing's equation and the symmetry of T^{ab}. A special case of this occurs when a spacetime is flat, so that the Levi-Civita derivative operator ∇_a is just a coordinate derivative operator ∂_a. In any case, not all spacetimes are stationary – that is, admit of a timelike KVF – which is why (the objection goes) conservation of energy–momentum holds only in such special cases.[23]

The authors of this sort of objection seem to assume that stationarity is *necessary* for conservation, in addition to it being sufficient (which is only what I maintain). Some examples show that this can't be right. Another sufficient condition for energy–momentum conservation is that energy–momentum vanishes: $T^{ab} = \mathbf{0}$. But such vacuum spacetimes in general will not be stationary. One could then retreat to the position that not stationarity, but the vanishing of either side of Eq. (14) in some way or other is what is necessary. However, yet another sufficient condition for energy–momentum conservation is that energy–momentum is covariantly constant: $\nabla_c T^{ab} = \mathbf{0}$. Note that the index on the derivative operator is not contracted with any of the energy–momentum tensor; since the former determines the notion of change in a GR model, this condition literally states that energy–momentum is not changing. Spacetimes with a covariantly constant but nonvanishing energy–momentum need not be stationary.

I suggest a different necessary and sufficient condition for conservation: For each $p \in M$ and timelike geodesic through p with tangent vector field ξ^a, the source density vanishes, $\nabla_a(T^{ab}\xi_b)_{|p} = \mathbf{0}$. The motivation behind this condition is twofold. First, the geodesics through p are the timelike components of the frames most analogous to the inertial ones familiar from flat spacetime (cf. Duerr 2019, 2). Second, while the exact value of the source density at p may vary from frame to frame, a true source cannot be made to vanish in a given frame. An analogy with electromagnetism is instructive: Although the charge

---

[22]　In fact, when the spacetime in question is asymptotically flat, an asymptotically timelike KVF will do, but this extension makes no difference in the arguments that follow.

[23]　Hoefer (2000) seems to demand the stronger condition that one be able to replace ∇_a with a coordinate derivative operator in the right-hand side of Eq. (14), but I do not see any justification for this aside from a syntactic analogy with prerelativistic physics.

density of an electromagnetic source will vary from frame to frame, it will never vanish in any frame unless it vanishes in all frames.

In any case, this condition is always satisfied in GR. The tangent vector fields ξ^a to the timelike geodesics through a point p are in fact *approximate* KVFs at p, meaning that $(\nabla_{(a}\xi_{b)})|_p = 0$, with the left-hand side varying smoothly in a neighborhood of p (Fletcher & Weatherall 2023a). Thus for such ξ^a, $\nabla_a(T^{ab}\xi_b)$ vanishes at p if and only if $\nabla_a T^{ab}$ vanishes at p. This comports with the fact that $\int_{\mathcal{U}} \nabla_a(T^{ab}\xi_b)\sigma$ can be made as small as one likes by selecting a sufficiently small neighborhood $\mathcal{U}$ of p (Hawking & Ellis 1973, 63) and suggests that this holds even if one normalized this integral by the volume of $\mathcal{U}$: The source density at p is truly zero.

4.3 Gravitational Energy

It is natural for students of elementary Newtonian gravitation to ask what the analogue of gravitational potential energy could be in GR. But, as one can gather from Sections 1 and 3.3, if gravitation in GR is just about the structure of space and time and gravity is not a matter field itself, then it should carry no associated energy–momentum, either as a source for the EFE or as a source of exchange for matter fields.[24] Nevertheless, it is instructive to consider some independent reasons for this conclusion.

Curiel (2019, §2) reviews the common argument pattern against there being a local concept of gravitational energy – one representable by a field on spacetime, such that the field values (or components of them) represent the energy content or density. This pattern invokes Einstein's principle of equivalence that gravitational effects are represented by the connection coefficients (Christoffel symbols) in some coordinate system. Because one can always select a coordinate system in which they vanish at a point, any energy attributable to them must vary similarly, but then it cannot be represented by a field, which does not so vary.

This argument assumes that the connection coefficients represent the gravitational field, which an advocate of gravitational energy may well reject in light of the argument (cf. Read 2020, 211). Curiel also relatedly and rightly objects that the argument assumes that whatever gravitational energy in GR could be, it must depend on the first derivatives of the metric (with respect to a flat coordinate derivative operator). Because gravitational phenomena are associated with the second derivatives through the Riemann curvature tensor,

---

[24] In fact, it is not often appreciated that gravitational energy encounters many of the same fraught issues in the Newtonian context (Dewar & Weatherall 2018).

the connection coefficients seem to be the wrong sort of mathematical object for the representational job.

Curiel (2019, §§6–7) provides a different argument that he interprets as proving the nonexistence of a gravitational energy–momentum tensor. In order for such a tensor to source the EFE, it must be a twice covariant symmetric tensor field. Further, it must be expressible as a sum of fields definable from the Riemann tensor, Ricci tensor, and the metric, such that it vanishes only if the Riemann tensor vanishes and is divergence-free in vacuum regions of spacetime. Finally, he requires that the tensor be invariant under any homothety $g_{ab} \mapsto \lambda g_{ab}$ for constant $\lambda > 0$, suggesting that this mapping represents a mere change in units. He then proves a theorem with a corollary stating that there is no tensor field satisfying all these constraints.

The theorem is in fact similar to one stated by Aldersley (1977) and later elaborated by Navarro and Sancho (2008) about the uniqueness of the EFE as a field equation. As Fletcher et al. (2018, §6.1) point out in the context of the discussion of these results, homothetic transformations represent *scale* transformations, not just changes in units. If the cosmological constant $\Lambda \neq 0$ or one considers any matter theories with intrinsic timescales or length scales, then one wouldn't expect such transformations to be symmetries as these results assume.[25] Accordingly, Curiel's argument is not as definitive as it might at first seem.

There is a different, simple argument against gravitational energy–momentum, due to Geroch and Malament in its original form (Dewar & Weatherall 2018, §1). (What follows is a slight variation on this form.) Recall that the two functions for energy–momentum, unified in GR, are to be the source for the EFE and to facilitate the description and explanation of the local dynamics of matter. First, suppose that gravity contributes as a source to the EFE. It must then be representable as a twice covariant tensor field. Then, in Ricci-flat, vacuum spacetimes (ones where $R_{ab} = 0$ and matter fields vanish), the gravitational energy–momentum is just Λg_{ab} (cf. Baker 2005). But this expression does not covary with the gravitational phenomena possible in such spacetimes, such as the presence of gravitational waves of various amplitudes. (I analyze the case of gravitational waves in more detail in the next subsection.)

---

[25] Curiel (2019) does acknowledge at least the point about the cosmological constant, countering that one must take Λg_{ab} to be simply the energy–momentum content of spacetime itself. (Aldersley [1977] and Navarro and Sancho [2008] counsel the same.) He does not acknowledge, however, the tension between affirming *spacetime* energy–momentum while denying *gravitational* energy–momentum. I discuss this option further in the remainder of this section.

So, if gravitational energy–momentum serves as a source in the EFE, it cannot in general satisfy its descriptive and explanatory functions for local dynamics.

Second, suppose that it does not serve as a source in the EFE. Could it still fulfill its local dynamical role? Since by assumption it is not a source in the EFE, while the energy–momentum T^{ab} of matter fields is, the latter by itself satisfies the conservation condition $\nabla_a T^{ab} = \mathbf{0}$. Because (as argued in the previous subsection) this is a legitimate expression of conservation, there is no energy–momentum exchange between matter and gravitation. Thus, if one aims for coordinate-free, frame-free descriptions and explanations of the local dynamics of matter, gravitational energy would play no role. One therefore reaches this same conclusion regardless of whether any putative gravitational energy–momentum is a source in the EFE.

This simple argument however leaves open the possibility that there are coordinate- or frame-relative (etc.) notions of gravitational energy–momentum. To see how these arise, suppose that one has committed to analyzing the local dynamics of a system in terms of some specific coordinate system or frame of reference. It could be the "laboratory" frame for a specific experiment or another constructed for some convenience or other. With respect to this local frame or coordinate system, there is a flat derivative operator, ∂_a, which is also the Levi-Civita derivative operator for any of a variety of only locally defined flat spacetime metrics. With respect to this operator, one may well find that $\partial_a T^{ab} \neq \mathbf{0}$, that is, when one constructs a notion of change for some more or less arbitrary coordinate system or frame, one may find with respect to it that the matter energy–momentum tensor is *not* divergence-free. The situation is analogous to the analysis of a classical mechanical material system in a noninertial frame or accelerating coordinate system: With respect to these, there are yet unaccounted-for coordinate accelerations, hence transfers of coordinate-based energy–momentum (Duerr 2019, 4). To restore coordinate-based energy conservation, one can describe the work done on the system through (fictitious) forces like the Coriolis force. In the context of GR, one can restore energy conservation with respect to the chosen coordinate system by describing a coordinate-dependent gravitational energy–momentum pseudotensor, $t^{\alpha\beta}$, so that $\partial_\alpha(\sqrt{|g|}(T^{\alpha\beta} + t^{\alpha\beta})) = 0$. The exchange between $T^{\alpha\beta}$ and $t^{\alpha\beta}$ expresses how the matter fields' behavior differs from that which would be expected if the metric were rather a flat metric to which the coordinate system or frame in question was adapted.

Notoriously, rather than there being a unique viable candidate for $t^{\alpha\beta}$, there is a proliferation of options, but there is some order to them: Each corresponds to a Lagrangian for gravity with respect to the aforementioned fixed flat metric, or alternatively, a certain expression of *Sparling's form* on the linear frame bundle on the spacetime manifold (Szabados 1992, 2009). In the latter case, the coordinate-dependence of $t^{\alpha\beta}$ results from pulling back Sparling's form along a particular coordinate section of the linear frame bundle; different coordinate sections are like different choices of gauge for a gauge theory. Thus, just as the energy–momentum tensor T^{ab} for matter is not a property of matter fields alone but in general depends also on the metric g_{ab} (Lehmkuhl 2011), any particular gravitational energy–momentum pseudotensor is relational – indeed, doubly so: first, to either a particular gravitational Lagrangian or a choice of the expression of Sparling's form, and second, to a particular coordinate system or frame field. This is exactly as one expects: With respect to a reference flat metric, the exact coordinate-dependent energetic properties of gravity will depend on its Lagrangian and the coordinates chart chosen. Descriptions and explanations of matter dynamics using this takes motion along coordinates adapted to the reference metric as default and assigns gravitational energy–momentum to capture departure from it.

Does $t^{\alpha\beta}$ represent a real property? There are at least three issues that bear on this question: (i) the dependence on a coordinate system or reference frame, (ii) the dependence on the gravitational Lagrangian or expression of Sparling's form, and (iii) the function to which $t^{\alpha\beta}$ is put. Coordinate or frame-dependence evinces a failure of definability unless the coordinate system or frame is given already from other fields, such as the comoving frame of certain matter fields, or added explicitly as auxiliary spacetime structure. A failure of definability does not necessarily entail meaninglessness, but at least it entails that the putative corresponding property is not represented in the spacetime model (cf. the haecceities involved in the hole argument discussed in Section 3.4). One way to ameliorate this is to consider at once all coordinate systems, as Pitts (2010) suggests, but it is unclear how the resulting object with uncountably infinitely many components will aid in the description and explanation of local matter dynamics without selecting a single component. But in applications where $t^{\alpha\beta}$ really facilitates description and explanation, the relevant frame is indeed determined from matter fields or added explicitly as a highly abstracted representation of a laboratory or other regions with measurement devices.

The second two issues (ii) and (iii) are, in my view, more serious threats to the reality of gravitational energy–momentum. Different equivalent Lagrangians for gravitation or expressions of one and the same Sparling's form on the frame bundle yield different $t^{\alpha\beta}$s. The gravitational energy–momentum realist would need to select one and thereby reify distinctions which are not otherwise of theoretical importance (much less being of any empirical significance). Further (and regarding the last issue (iii)), the sort of descriptions and explanations given are with respect to a representation of change (∂_a) that in general does not agree with the fundamental representation of change (∇_a), much in the way that straight-line motion in an accelerating frame of reference will not in general agree with straight-line motion in an inertial frame of reference. Read (2020, §3.3.3) suggests that one can reify $t^{\alpha\beta}$ because one can do so for any structure that plays a useful role in explanations, but in classical mechanics one does not reify fictitious forces just because they figure in descriptions and explanations from ballistics to meteorology.

Quantities or structures that depend on some frame determined by spacetime or matter structure and which avoid these issues (ii) and (iii) thus have more of a claim to represent a real property of spacetime. For example, Goswami and Ellis (2018) show that in spacetimes with certain symmetries, one can define a "square-root" of the Bel–Robinson tensor, which functions as a kind of energy–momentum tensor for "free gravity," the components of curvature represented in the Weyl tensor. Another example is that asymptotically flat spacetimes implicitly define a Minkowski metric to which the spacetime metric converges at infinity, in a sense that can be made precise (Wald 1984, Ch. 11). For such spacetimes, one can define an energy–momentum contained in entire spacelike slices. I discuss these latter examples more in the following subsection, after a longer case study of gravitational waves. (For more examples, see Szabados [2009].)

4.4 Gravitational Waves and Isolated Systems

If gravitational energy–momentum in GR has a status much like a fictitious force, as I argued in the previous subsection, how does one explain the manifest and measured effects of gravitational waves radiated from distant sources? In the first direct observation of gravitational waves, the Advanced LIGO experiment in 2015 detected the cataclysmic merger of a pair of black holes through its wave signal (Abbott et al. 2016). Much before then, in 1974, Russell Hulse and Joseph Taylor discovered a binary star system (now known as the Hulse–Taylor binary) consisting of a neutron star and a pulsar, the radio pulses of the latter fortuitously pointed towards Earth. GR predicts that the system slowly inspirals as it emits gravitational waves, equally slowly decreasing its orbital period. That's exactly what they observed, earning them the 1993 Nobel Prize in Physics. Data over several decades continues to fit the GR prediction well (Weisberg & Taylor 2005).

The modern theory of gravitational waves is vast and much of it subtle, but only a qualitative review is needed here. (For a standard presentation, see, e.g., Misner et al. [1973, Part VIII] or Wald [1984, Ch. 4.3b], which are briefer, while D'Ambrosio et al. [2022] is more thorough but pedagogical.)

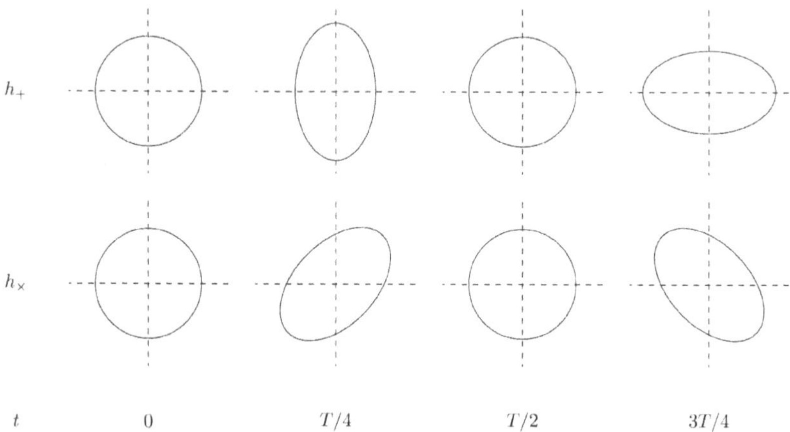

Figure 2 h_+ and $h_\times$ are the two dimensions of gravitational plane-wave polarizations at a given frequency. t depicts the portion of the period T. So, each row depicts stages in the evolution of a ring of test particles in a plane at the indicated polarization, as a gravitational wave passes in the direction normal to the ring.

There are at least two related sorts of approaches to gravitational waves and their radiative sources. The first approach decomposes the metric into a fixed part and a "perturbation" that, in some desired coordinate system, one takes to be small. One then *linearizes* the EFE to show that certain initial conditions for this perturbation yield a wave equation, with the quadrupole moment of rotating material bodies as the dominant source. The second, "shortwave" approach "grafts" a portion of a known exact plane-wave spacetime solution with a given wavelength onto a spacetime whose typical radius of curvature is much larger, then approximates the nonlinear interaction. Both are approximation (not idealization!) schemes that do not incur too much error in different overall circumstances. Essentially, both sorts of plane waves, which idealize this radiation far from its source, have a two-dimensional space of polarizations. Figure 2 depicts the effects of gravitational waves with these polarizations on a ring of test particles. It induces a periodic geodesic deviation in the particles.

Aptly for the present discussion, in the early history of GR, there was considerable controversy over whether gravitational waves exist and, if so, whether they "carry energy" (Kennefick 2019). Early researchers (including Einstein) were unclear about the distinction between wavelike phenomena and wavelike representations, the latter of which could be of non-wavelike phenomena. For instance, by a suitable choice of coordinates, even a massive test particle with a geodesic worldline in Minkowski spacetime can *appear* to follow a waving trajectory in those coordinates. Describing their effects

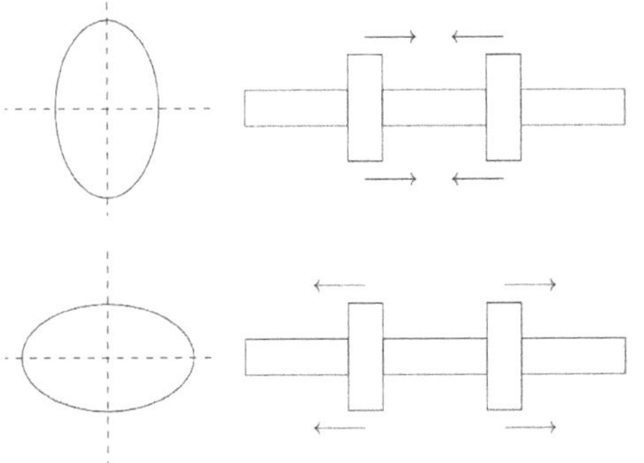
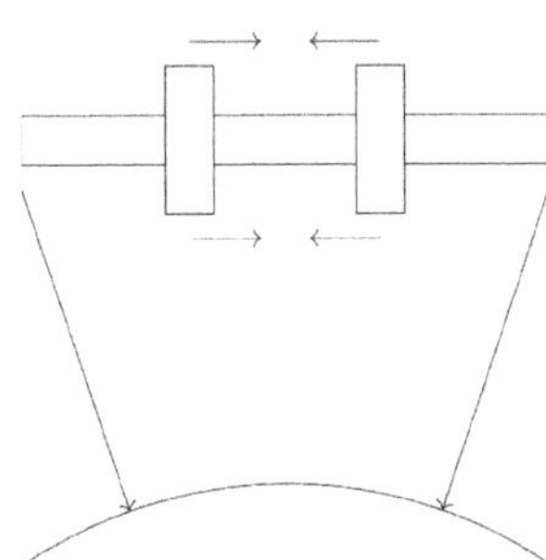

(a) The "sticky bead" thought experiment. The left-hand side of the diagram indicates the gravitational wave's effects on test particles at certain times in the period of evolution of the wave—cf. Figure 2; the right-hand side indicates the state of the beads on the bar immediately preceding those times, where the arrows indicate the relative acceleration of the beads to the bar. Friction between the beads and bar opposes these accelerations, thereby heating the system.

(b) The "falling bar" thought experiment. The bar with beads falls towards the center of a planet; the radial arrows depict the bar's relative acceleration. These arrows' components parallel to the bar yield a relative acceleration of the beads, depicted by the parallel arrows.

Figure 3 Comparison of the "sticky bead" and "falling bar" thought experiments.

in terms of frame-independent features, such as the geodesic deviation they induce, resolves this problem.

Felix Pirani was the first to explain this in 1956. Historically, though, the relativity community was focused on the energy question and so was convinced by a different sort of argument due to Richard Feynman and elaborated by Herman Bondi a couple of years later. Known as the "sticky bead" thought experiment, depicted in Figure 3(a), it asks one to consider a rigid rod with two ringlike beads that can slide with friction on the rod. As a gravitational wave front passes through, the beads will slide back and forth on the bar, and through the action of friction heat up the bar. Surely, the argument concludes, the bar can only heat up if the gravitational waves transfer energy to it. (Cf. the quotation from Rovelli [1997] about the rock of Gibralter in Section 3.3.) If this energy transfer is indispensable to this explanation, then it – hence local gravitational energy, fungible with thermodynamic energy – has a claim to reality. All this from the vacuum, naught but the unvanishing Weyl tensor.

The thought experiment may discomfit a skeptic of gravitational energy–momentum, but they may take a first step towards recovery by recognizing that its *dramatis personae* are distractingly specialized. First, and most importantly, one can realize the relevant sliding motion of the beads through any geodesic deviation. In Figure 3(b), the same bar and beads fall towards the center of a spherically symmetric planet. In the exterior Schwarzschild metric, the beads' inward geodesic deviation is a course in their natural motion towards the center of the planet. (If there is anything special about the waves, it is their especially long range, deriving from the exact plane-wave solution's Petrov type [N], compared with other effects.) Second, geodesic deviation does not require a nonvanishing Weyl tensor; to achieve the same result, one can replace the external Schwarzschild spacetime with one that is conformally flat, such as an expanding Friedmann–Lemaître–Robertson–Walker (FLRW) spacetime. Third, the frictional mechanism of temperature change is inessential: One can replace the bar and beads with a more thermodynamically familiar double-pistoned tube of gas. Instead of the beads sliding frictionally, the pistons compress or expand the gas.

One can analyze each of these thought experiments from at least two points of view in the theater of the mind. The first is that within a selected frame, which determines a flat derivative operator. According to it, one can assign a pseudotensor of energy–momentum to the gravitational wave or the gravity of the planet or the cosmos. Gravity then does work on beads, some of which converts to heat, or on the pistons, which adiabatically heat or cool the gas. Indeed, thermodynamics since Joule has been tempted to define work and heat through the equivalent ability to raise or lower a weight against a "uniform gravitational force," *presupposing the notions provided only through a flat derivative operator*. As descriptively convenient and useful as it is, however, the work done is as fictitious as the force from which it derives.

The second point of view stands in no frame. According to it, the bar does work on the beads, impeding their natural motion, some of which converts to heat; similarly, the gas does work on the pistons, impeding their natural inward motion. Gravitation, including gravitation waves, can facilitate real changes in motion and transformations of local thermodynamic quantities without the local addition or subtraction of energy encoded in T_{ab}.[26] That point of view sees no local gravitational energy, hence annuls the latter's claim to reality through explanatory indispensability.

Morals similar in some respects apply to the binary inspiral. The inspiral and the emission of gravitational waves are predictions of the EFE alone, confirmed through numerical simulation (cf. Dürr 2019, §3.3); no energy-based explanation is needed, hence no indispensability claim is substantiated. However, if one models the binary system as isolated, in an asymptotically flat spacetime, then this asymptotic flatness itself defines a flat derivative operator (or, rather, a class that are asymptotically equivalent) and a boundary at infinity. One can then integrate pseudotensorial energy–momentum quantities

---

[26] Thermodynamics does not usually countenance changes of state in a system without the system exchanging some extensive quantity, such as energy or momentum, with its environment. That thermodynamics without frames seems to demand this must await another occasion for analysis.

over a spacelike hypersurface extending to spatial infinity, and, incredibly, the result is independent of the particular pseudotensor and coordinate system used to express it. The resulting quantity, called the Arnowitt–Deser–Misner (ADM) energy–momentum, is in fact independent of the particular spatial hypersurface, as long as it extends to spatial infinity.[27] This means that the ADM energy–momentum is a global conserved quantity for isolated systems. If one picks a different type of spacelike hypersurface, asymptotic to future null infinity, one can arrive at a different quantity, the Bondi–Sachs energy–momentum. If a central, isolated body emits gravitational waves to future null infinity during an isolated period, one can sandwich this period between two such hypersurfaces. One will then find that the Bondi–Sachs energy–momentum decreases as a function of the gravitational wave flux (encoded in a technical construction called the Bondi news function). It is tempting to conclude from this that "*gravitational radiation always carries positive energy away from a radiating system*" (Wald 1984, 292), but we should not get carried away with interpreting this too literally: Gravitational radiation does not carry away energy in the way that one retrieves a concentrated deliciousness in curry from a takeaway. In the ordinary sense, the properties carried away are localized, but Bondi–Sachs energy–momentum is a global quantity not attributable to localized regions of spacetime. We can attribute this property to the gravitational waves in space at a time (i.e., on a spatial hypersurface) but not much more locally.

The conservation of ADM energy–momentum and its failure for Bondi–Sachs energy–momentum is less surprising when one reflects on what they represent. Each of them encodes how quickly curvature falls off as one reaches towards infinity from an isolated body, just as the total mass of a swarm of bodies in a Newtonian spacetime determines the falloff of their gravitational force on distant massive bodies. The ADM version selects a spacelike hypersurface that is guaranteed to slice through all persisting matter and radiation, while the Bondi–Sachs version picks a slice that does not intersect with radiation escaping to null infinity. For these reasons, they of course *must* be global quantities only defined for asymptotically flat spacetimes. But for the same reason, these global concepts of energy–momentum are not concepts of purely *gravitational* energy–momentum, for they are insensitive to whether the central body is material. Both a black hole and a material star with the same

---

27 Because of this, all that matters to the value of the ADM energy–momentum is how these quantities fall off towards infinity. Thus, it is possible to express the ADM energy–momentum as an integral over the spatial "boundary" at infinity, a set of ideal points defined by the asymptotically flat structure.

external Schwarzschild metric will yield the same global energy–momentum even though one is purely gravitational and the other material. For Bondi–Sachs energy–momentum, one can nevertheless distinguish the change due to gravitational wave flux and material (e.g., electromagnetic) flux.

In sum, the analysis of phenomena involving gravitational waves invokes two energy concepts, one local and the other global. The local one involves the same sort of relational quantities relative to some preferred frame or coordinate system discussed in Section 4.3, so what it represents will follow what the frame or system represents, just as in the case of fictitious forces in classical mechanics. It does not have any additional claim to reality in virtue of explanatory indispensability, as – despite its immense utility – it is in the end dispensable. The global concepts encode how curvature falls off to zero for an isolated system along different sorts of spatial slices. It is not a purely gravitational notion of energy, although the gravitational contribution to its change can be distinguished from the material contribution in the Bondi–Sachs case. The distribution of local, relational gravitational and material energy–momentum make a difference to it, but it is not fungible with them.

5 Time and Causality

5.1 Time and Time Travel

In most of prerelativistic physics, time manifests many familiar properties. One can locate every atomic event on a single timeline with a temporal metric. Thus, the duration of any process or history is determined entirely by the atomic events on its boundary. The timeline can be totally ordered, splitting all the rest, with respect to any atomic event, into past and future. In GR, these properties do not generally hold. As discussed in Section 1, the metric assigns a duration to every timelike curve – a one-dimensional process or history – which is *not* determined by the atomic events on the boundary of the curve. Consequently, it is never possible to locate all atomic events on a single timeline. Many (though not all) relativistic spacetimes still admit of a transitive ordering on their atomic events, however. This ordering, called a time orientation, can be specified in many ways (Minguzzi 2019, §1.7); perhaps the simplest is by a timelike vector field. At the tangent space of each point of the manifold, this field determines a vector in one of the two null cones, picking it out as the "future" direction: all timelike and null vectors lying in the same cone – those co-oriented with it – are said to be future-directed. (The rest are said to be past-directed.) One atomic event, q, is then to the future of another, p, if and only if there is a continuous timelike or null curve from p to q whose tangent vector field is future-directed.

There are some relativistic spacetimes that admit of structure with properties more analogous to those of time familiar from prerelativistic physics. For instance, a spacetime with manifold M *admits of a time function* when there is a continuous scalar field $t : M \to \mathbb{R}$ such that whenever q is to the future of p, $t(q) > t(p)$.[28] (t is said to be a *temporal* function if moreover t is at least once differentiable and is strictly increasing along all future directions.) Such a function assigns a kind of "time" to every atomic event, one that mirrors the temporal ordering of the orientation, thereby locating these events along a timeline. However, the times thereby assigned do not reflect any temporal metric; not all curves starting at $p \in M$ and ending in $q \in M$ have a duration $t(q) - t(p)$, and indeed it is possible that none do. Moreover, if a spacetime admits of one time (temporal) function, then it admits of infinitely many with different collections of level sets, the collections of atomic events assigned the same "time."

On occasion it is possible to select a unique time (temporal) function with distinguished properties (cf. Lachièze-Rey 2014, §5.3). In realistic FLRW models,[29] for example, which are the standard cosmological models, one can define the *cosmic time* function as that which assigns to any $p \in M$ the *supremum* of the durations of all future-directed continuous timelike curves ending at p. Cosmic time is always finite in such FLRW models (unlike, say, in Minkowski spacetime) because these models have a big bang singularity, meaning that *all* future-directed timelike curves with future endpoint have a finite duration. Moreover, the cosmic time of an atomic event within an FLRW model *is* equal to the duration of the worldline of a mote of eternal fluid ending in that event, for in FLRW models, the matter content of the universe is a homogeneous, isotropic perfect fluid. This fact undergirds empirical claims about the current age of the universe: They are just claims about the cosmic time of current events on Earth as if those events were occupied by such a mote. However, FLRW models are clearly idealized: The material content of the universe is not literally a homogeneous, isotropic perfect fluid. In any case, because the worldlines through the Earth never align with the geodesic congruence prescribed by the FLRW models, cosmic time does not track the durations we experience. Nor do the hypersurfaces of constant cosmic time match (except at a single atomic

---

[28] Admitting a time function is one condition in the middle of a linear hierarchy of conditions caused the "causal ladder" (Minguzzi 2019, §4), which characterize qualitatively how similar the global structure of time in a relativistic spacetime is to that of prerelativistic physics. For lack of space, I only discuss in this section the top (global hyperbolicity) and bottom couple of rungs (nontotal viciousness and chronology) of the ladder in addition to the middle.

[29] Here, "realistic" means that the perfect fluid source has everywhere positive density and nonnegative pressure, and the cosmological constant is not too large and negative (Hawking & Ellis 1973, 197).

event) the hypersurfaces of standard simultaneity given by any observer, even one comoving with the idealized perfect fluid.[30]

Just as some relativistic spacetimes admit of structure with properties more analogous to those of time familiar from prerelativistic physics, others have properties quite disanalogous. One of the most striking of these is the existence of closed timelike curves (CTCs), which are piecewise C^1 timelike curves that are not injective – they "close" back on themselves so that two distinct parameter values map to the same atomic event. A spacetime with manifold M is said to violate/satisfy *chronology* if and only if it does/does not contain a CTC. Clearly a spacetime violating chronology does not admit of a time (temporal) function. Any spacetime's *chronology-violating region* is the set $C \subseteq M$ through which a CTC passes. Spacetimes for which $C = M$ are said to be *totally vicious*. One can construct a simple example of a totally vicious spacetime by rolling up 2-d Minkowski spacetime along an adapted timelike coordinate. Not all CTCs arise from a nontrivial topology, however.[31] A famous early example is Gödel spacetime (Gödel 1949*a*, 2000) (for more on which, see Ellis and Krasiński [2000] and Malament [2012, Ch. 3.1]). Its spacetime manifold is diffeomorphic to $\mathbb{R}^4$. But not all spacetimes violating chronology are totally vicious. Misner and Taub-NUT spacetimes are so (Hawking & Ellis 1973, Ch. 5.8), as is the interior of Kerr spacetime (Hawking & Ellis 1973, Ch. 5.6).

CTCs are widely taken to be examples of time travel, as they represent processes or objects that loop back onto an atomic event in their past. Indeed, many authors *identify* CTCs with time travel in a relativistic spacetime (e.g., Visser 2003, Smeenk & Wüthrich 2011, 580). But this identification is too facile. Time travel involves, somehow, a local way in which the time experienced by the "traveler" is out of joint with the world around them. Looping processes or objects are clearly *one* but not the *only* way for time to be locally out of joint – consider, after all, the twins ("paradox") thought experiment (Smith 2021, §1): a traveler sets out from Earth for a round trip on a powerful rocket ship. When they return after, say, a few months' travel, they arrive in Earth's future 100 years hence, long after their twin has perished. There is a legitimate sense in which the traveler has indeed arrived at Earth's future without traversing any CTCs.

---

[30] These distinct types of spacelike hypersurfaces are sometimes known as *public space* (determined by cosmic time) and *private space* (determined by an individual worldline's standard simultaneity) (Malament 2007, 251). These various ways in which cosmic time does not capture the time of our experience play a role in my criticism of Lewis's definition of time travel, in the remainder of this section.

[31] In certain cases, some CTCs must arise: If M is compact, then $C \neq \emptyset$ (Hawking & Ellis 1973, Prop. 6.4.2).

Perhaps a clearheaded definition of time travel will encompass CTCs and the twins. The most popular definition is due to David Lewis (1976, 145–146): One is a time traveler when one's personal time does not match external, objective time. In particular, one travels to the future on a journey when one's personal duration is shorter than the external duration of the journey; one travels to the past when one arrives at an external time earlier than when one started. But as I reviewed previously in this section, relativistic spacetimes do not generally admit of anything like an external time that determines the time elapsed between two atomic events. To overcome this, Fano and Macchia (2020) appeal to the best-case scenario of a cosmological FLRW model with cosmic time and suggest somehow embedding any local model with time travel, such as the interior Kerr metric, as a separate model into the FLRW model. Mathematically, this is not possible while preserving a well-defined cosmic time. But they affirm that this superposition is contradictory "only if the following metaphysical principle, which we can call *property transmission from whole to parts*, holds: If one object O has the property A and o is a proper part of O and A is incompatible with the property B, then o could not have B" (Fano & Macchia 2020, 4863–4864). They reject this principle; but it is rather *sufficient*, not necessary for contradiction, as they insist. Contradiction here arises not from principles metaphysical, but mathematical. Even if this could be assuaged somehow, because the Earth's time does not match cosmic time – it is in motion relative to the average motion of matter in the universe – anything on Earth will always count as a time traveler, for the usual time dilation reasons. Cosmic time as Lewisian external time thus yields the wrong verdicts about what and who are time travelers.

Daniels (2014, 339, 343) has made a different proposal for adapting Lewis's definition to the relativistic context: "An object, O, is a time traveller *iff* there is another frame wherein an object would have a different proper time from s to e than O," where s and e are the starting and ending achronal hypersurfaces, respectively, for O. Unfortunately this proposal is not conceptually or mathematically consistent: The presupposed achronal hypersurfaces may not exist (e.g., in Gödel spacetime) and there is a conflation of properties of proper time with properties of frame-based coordinate time assignments. Proper times are not frame-dependent, so presumably Daniels intends to refer to frame-based temporal coordinate assignments, which differ from an object's proper time. But there will always be such frames, so whenever s and e exist, an object with a worldline through them will be a time traveller. Daniels (2014, 339–341) acknowledges this, affirming that not all time travelers will be "philosophically interesting," an analysis of which he declines. The issue, however, is that the proposed definition of time travel is trivial: It is extensionally equivalent (where it applies) to other trivial properties such as being self-identical, so it is difficult to see how it provides insight into the phenomenon of time travel.

Arntzenius (2006, 603) proposed a variation on this idea restricted to backwards time travel:

> Suppose there is some (connected, 4-dimensional) sub-region R of space-time which one can slice up into time-slices, so that one can define an external time confined to R. Now suppose that there is a person whose world-line W partially lies in R. Then we can say that person P travels back in time if there are events A and B such that according to P's personal time A occurs before B while according to R's external time B occurs before A.

The "slic[ing] up into time-slices" is essentially just the assignment of a time function to the region R. This proposal, as far as it goes, does not have the disadvantages of Daniels's, but its scope is limited in two ways: It does not capture time travel to the future, nor does it offer any quantitative assessment of *how far* in time a time traveler has traveled. Arntzenius (2006, 605) acknowledges the former, but demurs that it would encounter the same sort of triviality problem that afflicts Daniels's:

> According to (special and general) relativity two clocks that travel along different world-lines from space-time point A to space-time point B will, almost always, measure different time intervals between A and B no matter what the structure the space-time has. . . . So, on a fairly natural characterization of what it is for there to be forwards time travel, forwards time travel would be ubiquitous, too ubiquitous to be interesting.

Arntzenius (2006, 605) admits that perhaps there is some way of capturing a nontrivial sense of relativistic time travel to the future, but does not pursue it.

It is worth pursuing briefly here by combining certain aspects of Arntzenius's and Daniels's proposals. Abstracting from both, the essential idea in Lewis's invocation of "external" time is not that it is object- or frame-independent, but rather that it can provide a *normality* standard for determining when some personal time (along a worldline, say) is out of joint. From Arntzenius, I take the idea that this normality standard should be a *local* time function, that is, one defined on only a portion of spacetime. From Daniels, I take the idea that there needn't be a single, uniquely defined normality standard. The new ingredient I add is some measure of *how* abnormally out of joint some personal time is, attributing time travel only to those whose personal time is sufficiently abnormal, which I allow to be contextually determined. With these inputs, I arrive at the following schema:

> Let a relativistic spacetime with manifold M be given, as well as a timelike worldline $O : I \to M$ parameterized by arc length (with $I \subseteq \mathbb{R}$ an interval), a countable sequence of local time functions $t_i : U_i \to \mathbb{R}$ with $U_i \subseteq M$ and $O[I] \subseteq \bigcup_i U_i$, a discrepancy measure $d : \mathbb{R} \times \mathbb{R} \to \mathbb{R}$, which is a signed distance function, and a real number $\epsilon \geq 0$. Further assume that the local time functions are sequentially compatible, i.e., $t_i(p) = t_{i+1}(p)$ where defined. Then O time travels relative to t, d, and ϵ at $p \in O[I]$ iff $d(O^{-1}[p], t(p)) > \epsilon$, where $d(O^{-1}[p], t(p))$ gives the time discrepancy at p.

In a word, time travel occurs for O in U when the time experienced by O differs from that given by t_i by more than ϵ according to the discrepancy measure d. Whether any instantiation and application of this scheme to a particular case is interesting will depend on the relevance of the standard of temporal normality (t_i) and precision (d) to that case as well as the particular parameterization I. In many cases of interest, there will be a single t generated by some local congruence of timelike geodesics, I will in some way cohere with some of the assignments of t, d will be the difference function, and ϵ will be some threshold of practical imperceptibility. For instance, in the case of the twins thought experiment, t will be given by some local Newtonian model for a spacetime tube surrounding the Earth, I will initially cohere with t before the traveling twin's journey, and d and ϵ will be as just indicated.

An interesting advantage of this definition of time travel is that it suggests a classification thereof based on how time discrepancies arise. For instance, one can select d so that time travel to the future/past arises as the (greater than ϵ) time discrepancy is positive/negative, with the magnitude describing how "far" the travel extends. Moreover, one can identify time travel arising because of temporal loops by when the local time functions t_i do not effectively piecewise define a single local time function. Perhaps other fruitful classifications are possible.

Most philosophical discussions of time travel's implications for the nature of time or matter, such as for the debate between presentists, who maintain that only the present is real, and eternalists, who maintain that the past, present, and future are equally real, do not draw from GR (Smith 2021, §4). Because time travel in GR has typically been equated with CTCs, almost all of the discussion of these specific implications has focused on the seeming causal circularity of events thereon. Two exceptions to these trends have been Gödel's argument for the "ideality" of time, and an argument of my own concerning the ontology of matter (Fletcher 2020c).[32] For lack of space, I discuss only the former.

---

[32] My argument interrogates the interpretation of test particles by showing that they generate problems for **Histories** in spacetimes with closed timelike curves.

Drawing from his solution to the EFE containing CTCs discussed earlier in this section, Gödel (1949*b*, 562) argued:

> The mere compatibility with the laws of nature of worlds in which there is no distinguished absolute time, and, therefore, no objective lapse of time can exist, throws some light on the meaning of time in those worlds in which an absolute time *can* be defined. For, if someone asserts that this absolute time is lapsing, he accepts as a consequence that whether or not an objective lapse of time exists . . . depends on the particular way in which matter and its motion are arranged in the world. This is not a straightforward contradiction; nevertheless a philosophical view leading to such consequences can hardly be considered as satisfactory.

To understand what Gödel might have had in mind here, note that a typical model of GR does not contain as part of its auxiliary spacetime structure a distinguished time slice representing the global present, and so does not explicitly represent how that present could flow or change. Can one merely add this auxiliary structure just as one might add, say, a temporal orientation? A necessary condition for this is that a spacetime admit of a global time function. Spacetimes with CTCs, like Gödel spacetime, show that it's possible for spacetime not to admit of a global time function, hence not have a global objective time lapse. Finally, it is not "satisfactory" for this to be a contingent feature of a universe.

The last, modal step of Gödel's argument has been controversial, failing to convince most readers: Why shouldn't the global passage of time be a contingent feature of the universe? (See Earman [1995, 194–200], Smeenk and Wüthrich [2011, §4], and references therein for a detailed discussion.) However, there is a two-part elaboration that restores the argument's force (setting aside whether it is what Gödel intended), whose second part is original as far as I am aware. The first part relies on the concept of *(weak) observational indistinguishability*. A spacetime with manifold M is (weakly) observationally indistinguishable from a spacetime with manifold M' if for every $p \in M$ there is some $p' \in M'$ such that the pasts of p and p' are isometric. Call the spacetime with manifold M' a *nemesis* for the *original* spacetime with manifold M. Manchak (2016) proves that every original has a nemesis with the same manifold that does not admit a global time function, and that moreover the spacetime region in the nemesis that obstructs the existence of the time function may be chosen to lie in the future of any chosen point p of the original (rather than, say, being spacelike related to p). This entails that there can be no unequivocal evidence from physical experience for global objective time lapse. The second part marshals a standard Occamist norm against postulating surplus physical or metaphysical structure, all else being equal. From the first part, it does seem that, at least empirically, all else is equal regarding whether one postulates a global objective lapse of time, so one should not postulate it. The Occamist norm is not a conceptual truth, of course, so the defender of global objective time lapse can reject it, but doing so can hardly be considered as satisfactory, methodologically.[33]

5.2 Relativistic Causality

One of the first slogans one learns about relativity is that it prohibits superluminal signals, or influences, or propagation of matter. It is natural to read this as a sort of causality requirement or principle in the theory. What exactly is the nature and status of this prohibition (if it is not just a restatement of **Histories**, discussed in Section 1)? Consider the following definition of "local causality" from Hawking and Ellis (1973, 60):

> The equations governing the matter fields must be such that if U is a convex normal neighborhood and p and q are points in U then a signal can be sent in U between p and q if and only if p and q can be joined by a C^1 curve lying entirely in U, whose tangent vector is everywhere nonzero and is either timelike or null;. . ..
>
> A more precise statement of this postulate can be given in terms of the Cauchy problem of the matter fields. Let $p \in U$ be such that every [inextendible] non-spacelike curve through p intersects the spacelike surface $x^4 = 0$ within U. Let $\mathcal{F}$ be the set of points in the surface $x^4 = 0$ which can be reached by non-spacelike curves in U from p. Then we require that the values of the matter fields at p must be uniquely determined by the values of the fields and their derivatives up to some finite order on $\mathcal{F}$, and that they are not uniquely determined by the values on any proper subset of $\mathcal{F}$ to which it can be continuously retracted.

This passage is remarkable for its seemingly wild combination of ideas. What should the ostensibly anthropocentric idea of "signals" have to do with the structure of space, time, and matter? How could a local statement of determinism for matter be a more precise expression of this idea?

The semantic connotation of "signal" perhaps misleads; it denotes here more narrowly a propagating disturbance in a material medium. One way to make this idea precise is in terms of counterfactual difference-making (Weinstein 2006): Given a difference in the initial conditions of the medium, find whether these differences entail differences at events spacelike related from the initial

---

[33] A *local* objective time lapse may nevertheless be compatible with the argument; see Aames (2022) for a recent defense.

conditions. And here the connection with the Cauchy problem is evident. Earman (2014, 103) gives this a more precise formulation:[34]

> For any initial value hypersurface S and any initial datum Φ_0 on S
>
> (1) there is an open neighborhood U of S and a solution Φ of the field equations on U that agrees with Φ_0, and
> (2) for any point $p \in U$ if p belongs to the domain of dependence $D(A)$ of a closed subset A of S, then for any solutions Φ and Φ' on U that agree with Φ_0 on A, $\Phi(p) = \Phi'(p)$.

The *domain of dependence* of a set A is the points p of M such that all non-spacelike inextendible curves through p intersect A. In causal terms, it is the set of events that A determines, insofar as that determination follows timelike and null curves.

When the matter fields satisfy wavelike equations of motion – in technical terms, they are hyperbolic partial differential equations (Geroch 1996, Bär et al. 2007) – this characterization is equivalent to another in terms of those equations' *characteristic cones*. These are cones in the tangent space, much like the null cones of the spacetime metric, that specify the possible directions in spacetime for how a jump discontinuity in the fields governed by the equations in question propagates.[35] Consequently, if such a discontinuity in initial data represents an induced difference in the field medium, then one can track the characteristic surface it induces, which will always be in the domain of dependence of the initial dataset if the characteristic cones always lie within the null cones at all events in that domain (Weatherall 2014).[36] Indeed, "The requirement that the matter equations should be second order hyperbolic or first order hyperbolic systems with their cones coinciding with or lying within that of the space-time metric **g**, may be thought of as a more rigorous form of the local causality postulate" (Hawking & Ellis 1973, 255).

One of the remarkable features of local causality is that it is not a consequence of other assumptions of GR, and places no restrictions on spatiotemporal structure. It is rather an assumption about matter fields (about which Hawking and Ellis [1973, 60] are entirely forthcoming), one that ensures that the structure of those fields' causal dependence falls along relations of timelike or null dependence. Matter fields that do not satisfy it are nevertheless perfectly compatible with GR (Geroch 2011). For instance, Weatherall

---

[34] See also Wald (1984, 244).

[35] In fact, from a mathematical perspective, the null cones are also characteristic cones (Geroch 2011).

[36] Weinstein (2006, §2) complained that it would not be productive in general to try to find the worldline of a "signal" in trying to make relativistic causality precise, but this discussion shows that for wavelike phenomena, it can be made precise.

(2014, §5) shows how the characteristic cones for Maxwell equations for electromagnetism lie outside the null cones when traveling through a medium with (light frequency-independent) index of refraction $n < 1$. This does not of course mean that realistic matter can be found with this property. If one assumes instead that n depends on frequency such that $n \to 1$ as the frequency becomes arbitrarily large, then light's characteristic cones will lie inside the null cones. And this, in turn, is usually justified heuristically by appeal to the atomic theory of matter (Weatherall 2014, §6).

Sometimes one finds an alternative conception of relativistic causality for classical matter fields. According to it, that a field $\mathcal{F}$ satisfies **DEC** means that "the energy of $\mathcal{F}$ does not propagate with superluminal velocity" (Malament 2012, 144).[37] There are two facts often cited in support of this conception. First, as I stated before, since **DEC** entails that $T^{ab}\xi_b$ is non-spacelike for any timelike ξ^a, it entails that according to any frame, the flux density of net energy–momentum is non-spacelike. Second, Hawking and Ellis (1973, 94) prove a ("conservation") theorem that has as a consequence the fact that if the energy–momentum tensor (or, really, any divergence-free tensor) satisfies **DEC** and vanishes on a certain set A, then it also vanishes on $D(A)$. For fields that satisfy **AFHE**, "This result may be interpreted as saying that the dominant energy condition implies that matter cannot travel faster than light" (Hawking & Ellis 1973, 94) – or, really, that it cannot encroach into the vacuum faster than light.

The **DEC**, however, does not *characterize* relativistic causality because, while it is *sufficient* for the just mentioned consequences presented in favor of this characterization, it is not *necessary* for those consequences, nor is it necessary for the characterization endorsed before in this subsection. For instance, the Klein–Gordon field with a negative potential satisfies a hyperbolic equation of motion, but not the **DEC** (Earman 2014, 104). The failure of the **DEC** does not therefore *entail* any superluminal propagation of matter or energy, into the vacuum or otherwise. (In any case, the speed of vacuum encroachment does not entail anything about the speed of propagation in a nonvanishing medium – see Wong [2011] for examples and details.)

---

[37] See also Wald (1984, 219).

References

Aames, J. (2022), "Temporal becoming in a relativistic universe: Causal diamonds and Gödel's philosophy of time," *European Journal for Philosophy of Science* **12**(3), 1–24.

Abbott, B. P., Abbott, R., Abbott, T., et al. (2016), "Observation of gravitational waves from a binary black hole merger," *Physical Review Letters* **116**(6), 061102.

Adlam, E., Linnemann, N., & Read, J. (2022), "Constructive axiomatics in spacetime physics, part II: Constructive axiomatics in context," arXiv preprint arXiv:2211.05672.

Aghanim, N., Akrami, Y., Ashdown, M., et al. (2020), "Planck 2018 results–VI: Cosmological parameters," *Astronomy & Astrophysics* **641**, A6.

Aldersley, S. (1977), "Dimensional analysis in relativistic gravitational theories," *Physical Review D* **15**(2), 370.

Anderson, J. L. (1967), *Principles of Relativity Physics*, Academic Press.

Arntzenius, F. (2006), "Time travel: Double your fun," *Philosophy Compass* **1**(6), 599–616.

Ashby, N. (2003), "Relativity in the global positioning system," *Living Reviews in Relativity* **6**(1), 1–42.

Baez, J. C. & Bunn, E. F. (2005), "The meaning of Einstein's equation," *American Journal of Physics* **73**(7), 644–652.

Baker, D. J. (2005), "Spacetime substantivalism and Einstein's cosmological constant," *Philosophy of Science* **72**(5), 1299–1311.

Baker, D. J. (2021), "Knox's inertial spacetime functionalism," *Synthese* **199**(S2), 277–298.

Baker, M. R., Linnemann, N., & Smeenk, C. (2022), "Noether's first theorem and the energy-momentum tensor ambiguity problem," *in* J. Read & N. J. Teh, eds., *The Philosophy and Physics of Noether's Theorems: A Centenary Volume*, Cambridge University Press, pp. 169–196.

Bär, C., Ginoux, N., & Pfäffle, F. (2007), *Wave Equations on Lorentzian Manifolds and Quantization*, European Mathematical Society.

Barcelo, C. & Visser, M. (2002), "Twilight for the energy conditions?" *International Journal of Modern Physics D* **11**(10), 1553–1560.

Belot, G. (1995), "New work for counterpart theorists: Determinism," *The British Journal for the Philosophy of Science* **46**(2), 185–195.

Bianchi, E. & Rovelli, C. (2010), "Why all these prejudices against a constant?" arXiv preprint arXiv:1002.3966.

Brown, H. R. (2005), *Physical Relativity: Space-Time Structure from a Dynamical Perspective*, Oxford University Press.

Brown, H. R. (2018), "The behaviour of rods and clocks in general relativity and the meaning of the metric field," *in* D. E. Rowe, T. Sauer, & S. A. Walter, eds., *Beyond Einstein: Perspectives on Geometry, Gravitation, and Cosmology in the Twentieth Century*, Birkhäuser, pp. 51–66.

Brown, H. R. & Pooley, O. (2001), "The origin of the spacetime metric: Bell's 'Lorentzian pedagogy' and its significance in general relativity," *in* C. Callender & N. Huggett, eds., *Physics Meets Philosophy at the Planck Scale*, Cambridge University Press, pp. 256–272.

Brown, H. R. & Pooley, O. (2006), "Minkowski space-time: A glorious non-entity," *in* D. Dieks, ed., *The Ontology of Spacetime*, Elsevier, pp. 67–89.

Brown, J. R. & Fehige, Y. (2022), "Thought experiments," *in* E. N. Zalta, ed., *The Stanford Encyclopedia of Philosophy*, Spring 2022 ed., Metaphysics Research Lab, Stanford University.

Butterfield, J. (1989), "The hole truth," *The British Journal for the Philosophy of Science* **40**(1), 1–28.

Coffey, K. (2014), "Theoretical equivalence as interpretative equivalence," *The British Journal for the Philosophy of Science* **65**(4), 821–844.

Crelinsten, J. (2006), *Einstein's Jury: The Race to Test Relativity*, Princeton University Press.

Curiel, E. (2009), "General relativity needs no interpretation," *Philosophy of Science* **76**(1), 44–72.

Curiel, E. (2017), "A primer on energy conditions," *in* D. Lehmkuhl, G. Schiemann, & E. Scholz, eds., *Towards a Theory of Spacetime Theories*, Birkhäuser, pp. 43–104.

Curiel, E. (2019), "On geometric objects, the non-existence of a gravitational stress-energy tensor, and the uniqueness of the Einstein field equation," *Studies in History and Philosophy of Modern Physics* **66**, 90–102.

D'Ambrosio, F., Fell, S. D., Heisenberg, L., et al. (2022), "Gravitational waves in full, non-linear general relativity," arXiv preprint arXiv:2201.11634.

Daniels, N. (2020), "Reflective equilibrium," *in* E. N. Zalta, ed., *The Stanford Encyclopedia of Philosophy*, Summer 2020 ed., Metaphysics Research Lab, Stanford University.

Daniels, P. R. (2014), "Lewisian time travel in a relativistic setting," *Metaphysica* **15**(2), 329–345.

Dewar, N. & Weatherall, J. O. (2018), "On gravitational energy in Newtonian theories," *Foundations of Physics* **48**(5), 558–578.

Doboszewski, J. (2019), "Relativistic spacetimes and definitions of determinism," *European Journal for Philosophy of Science* **9**(2), 1–14.

Duerr, P. M. (2019), "Fantastic beasts and where (not) to find them: Local gravitational energy and energy conservation in general relativity," *Studies in History and Philosophy of Modern Physics* **65**, 1–14.

Duncan, A. & Janssen, M. (2022), "Quantization conditions, 1900–1927," *in* O. Freire Jr., ed., *The Oxford Handbook of the History of Quantum Interpretations*, Oxford University Press, pp. 77–94.

Dürr, P. M. (2019), "It ain't necessarily so: Gravitational waves and energy transport," *Studies in History and Philosophy of Modern Physics* **65**, 25–40.

Earman, J. (1995), *Bangs, Crunches, Whimpers, and Shrieks: Singularities and Acausalities in Relativistic Spacetimes*, Oxford University Press.

Earman, J. (2001), "Lambda: The constant that refuses to die," *Archive for History of Exact Sciences* **55**(3), 189–220.

Earman, J. (2003), "The cosmological constant, the fate of the universe, unimodular gravity, and all that," *Studies in History and Philosophy of Modern Physics* **34**(4), 559–577.

Earman, J. (2014), "No superluminal propagation for classical relativistic and relativistic quantum fields," *Studies in History and Philosophy of Modern Physics* **48**(2), 102–108.

Earman, J. & Norton, J. (1987), "What price spacetime substantivalism? The hole story," *The British Journal for the Philosophy of Science* **38**(4), 515–525.

Eddington, A. S. (1965), *The Mathematical Theory of Relativity*, 2nd ed., Cambridge University Press.

Ehlers, J. (1973), "Survey of general relativity theory," *in* W. Israel, ed., *Relativity, Astrophysics and Cosmology*, D. Reidel, pp. 1–125.

Ehlers, J., Pirani, F. A., & Schild, A. (1972), "The geometry of free fall and light propagation," *in* L. O'Reifeartaigh, ed., *General Relativity, Papers in Honour of J. L. Synge*, Clarendon Press, pp. 63–84.

Ehlers, J., Pirani, F. A., & Schild, A. (2012), "Republication of: The geometry of free fall and light propagation," *General Relativity and Gravitation* **44**(6), 1587–1609.

Einstein, A. (1923/1905), "On the electrodynamics of moving bodies," *in* *The Principle of Relativity*, Methuen, chapter III, pp. 35–65. Translated by George Barker Jeffery and Wilfrid Perrett.

Ellis, G. F. R. & Krasiński, A. (2000), "Editor's note: An example of a new type of cosmological solutions of Einstein's field equations of gravitation," *General Relativity and Gravitation* **32**(7), 1399–1408.

Fano, V. & Macchia, G. (2020), "A physical interpretation of Lewis? Discrepancy between personal and external time in time travels," *Synthese* **197**(11), 4847–4866.

Faye, J. (2019), "Copenhagen interpretation of quantum mechanics," *in* E. N. Zalta, ed., *The Stanford Encyclopedia of Philosophy*, Winter 2019 ed., Metaphysics Research Lab, Stanford University.

Fletcher, S. C. (2013), "Light clocks and the clock hypothesis," *Foundations of Physics* **43**(11), 1369–1383.

Fletcher, S. C. (2019), "On the reduction of general relativity to Newtonian gravitation," *Studies in History and Philosophy of Modern Physics* **68**, 1–15.

Fletcher, S. C. (2020*a*), "Approximate local Poincaré spacetime symmetry in general relativity," *in* C. Beisbart, T. Sauer, & C. Wüthrich, eds., *Thinking about Space and Time*, Springer, pp. 247–267.

Fletcher, S. C. (2020*b*), "On representational capacities, with an application to general relativity," *Foundations of Physics* **50**(4), 228–249.

Fletcher, S. C. (2020*c*), "Which worldlines represent possible particle histories?" *Foundations of Physics* **50**(6), 582–599.

Fletcher, S. C. (2021*a*), "Counterfactual reasoning within physical theories," *Synthese* **198**(16), 3877–3898.

Fletcher, S. C. (2021*b*), "Relativistic spacetime structure," *in* E. Knox & A. Wilson, eds., *The Routledge Companion to Philosophy of Physics*, Routledge, pp. 160–179.

Fletcher, S. C., Manchak, J., Schneider, M. D., & Weatherall, J. O. (2018), "Would two dimensions be world enough for spacetime?" *Studies in History and Philosophy of Modern Physics* **63**, 100–113.

Fletcher, S. C. & Weatherall, J. O. (2023*a*), "The local validity of special relativity, part 1: Geometry," *Philosophy of Physics* **1**(1), 7.

Fletcher, S. C. & Weatherall, J. O. (2023*b*), "The local validity of special relativity, part 2: Matter dynamics," *Philosophy of Physics* **1**(1), 8.

Frigg, R. & Hartmann, S. (2020), "Models in Science," *in* E. N. Zalta, ed., *The Stanford Encyclopedia of Philosophy*, Spring 2020 ed., Metaphysics Research Lab, Stanford University.

Frigg, R. & Nguyen, J. (2021), "Scientific Representation," *in* E. N. Zalta, ed., *The Stanford Encyclopedia of Philosophy*, Winter 2021 ed., Metaphysics Research Lab, Stanford University.

Geroch, R. (1971), "Space-time structure from a global viewpoint," *in* R. K. Sachs, ed., *General Relativity and Cosmology*, Academic Press, pp. 71–103.

Geroch, R. (1978), *General Relativity from A to B*, University of Chicago Press.

Geroch, R. (1996), "Partial differential equations of physics," *in* G. Hall & J. Pulham, eds., *General Relativity: Proceedings of the Forty Sixth Scottish Universities Summer School in Physics*, SUSSP, pp. 19–60.

Geroch, R. (2011), "Faster than light?, *in* M. Plaue, A. Rendall, & M. Scherfner, eds., *Advances in Lorentzian Geometry: Proceedings of the Lorentzian*

Geometry Conference in Berlin, Vol. 49 of *Studies in Advanced Mathematics*, American Mathematical Society and International Press, pp. 59–70.

Geroch, R. & Weatherall, J. O. (2018), "The motion of small bodies in spacetime," *Communications in Mathematical Physics* **364**(2), 607–634.

Geroch, R. P. & Horowitz, G. (1979), "Global structure of spacetimes," *in* S. W. Hawking & W. Israel, eds., *General Relativity: An Einstein Centenary Survey*, Cambridge University Press, pp. 212–293.

Gödel, K. (1949*a*), "An example of a new type of cosmological solutions of Einstein's field equations of gravitation," *Reviews of Modern Physics* **21**(3), 447.

Gödel, K. (1949*b*), "A remark about the relationship between relativity theory and idealistic philosophy," *in* P. A. Schilpp, ed., *Albert Einstein: Philosopher-Scientist*, Library of Living Philosophers, Northwestern University Press, pp. 555–562.

Gödel, K. (2000), "An example of a new type of cosmological solutions of Einstein's field equations of gravitation," *General Relativity and Gravitation* **32**(7), 1409–1417.

Goswami, R. & Ellis, G. F. R. (2018), "Transferring energy in general relativity," *Classical and Quantum Gravity* **35**(16), 165007.

Hagar, A. & Hemmo, M. (2013), "The primacy of geometry," *Studies in History and Philosophy of Modern Physics* **44**(3), 357–364.

Hawking, S. W. & Ellis, G. F. R. (1973), *The Large Scale Structure of Space-Time*, Cambridge University Press.

Hoefer, C. (2000), "Energy conservation in GTR," *Studies in History and Philosophy of Modern Physics* **31**(2), 187–199.

Hoefer, C. (2016), "Causal determinism," *in* E. N. Zalta, ed., *The Stanford Encyclopedia of Philosophy*, Spring 2016 ed., Metaphysics Research Lab, Stanford University.

Hohmann, M. (2014), "Aspects of multimetric gravity," *Journal of Physics: Conference Series* **532**, 012009.

Hojman, S. A. (2018), "Proper time redefined," *Physical Review D* **98**, 084037.

Hossenfelder, S. (2008), "Bimetric theory with exchange symmetry," *Physical Review D* **78**(4), 044015.

Kennefick, D. (2019), *No Shadow of a Doubt: The 1919 Eclipse that Confirmed Einstein's Theory of Relativity*, Princeton University Press.

Knox, E. (2010), "Flavour-oscillation clocks and the geometricity of general relativity," *The British Journal for the Philosophy of Science* **61**(2), 433–452.

Knox, E. (2019), "Physical relativity from a functionalist perspective," *Studies in History and Philosophy of Modern Physics* **67**, 118–124.

Koberinski, A. (2021), "Problems with the cosmological constant problem," *in* C. Wüthrich, B. Le Bihan, & N. Huggett, eds., *Philosophy beyond Spacetime*, Oxford University Press, pp. 260–280.

Lachièze-Rey, M. (2014), "In search of relativistic time," *Studies in History and Philosophy of Modern Physics* **46**, 38–47.

Lam, V. (2011), "Gravitational and nongravitational energy: The need for background structures," *Philosophy of Science* **78**(5), 1012–1023.

Landsman, K. (2022), *Foundations of General Relativity: From Einstein to Black Holes*, 2nd ed., Radboud University Press.

Lehmkuhl, D. (2008), "Is spacetime a gravitational field?" *in* D. Dieks, ed., *The Ontology of Spacetime II*, Vol. 4 of *Philosophy and Foundations of Physics*, Elsevier, pp. 83–110.

Lehmkuhl, D. (2011), "Mass–energy–momentum: Only there because of spacetime?" *The British Journal for the Philosophy of Science* **62**(3), 453–488.

Lehmkuhl, D. (2018), "The metaphysics of super-substantivalism," *Noûs* **52**(1), 24–46.

Lehmkuhl, D., Schiemann, G., & Scholz, E., eds. (2016), *Towards a Theory of Spacetime Theories*, Birkhäuser.

Lewis, D. (1976), "The paradoxes of time travel," *American Philosophical Quarterly* **13**(2), 145–152.

Lucas, J. R. (1973), *A Treatise on Time and Space*, Methuen.

Mainwaring, S. R. & Stedman, G. E. (1993), "Accelerated clock principles in special relativity," *Physical Review A* **47**, 3611–3619.

Malament, D. B. (2007), "Classical relativity theory," *in* J. Butterfield & J. Earman, eds., *Philosophy of Physics*, Vol. A of *Handbook of the Philosophy of Science*, North-Holland, pp. 229–275.

Malament, D. B. (2012), *Topics in the Foundations of General Relativity and Newtonian Gravitation Theory*, University of Chicago Press.

Manchak, J. B. (2016), "On Gödel and the ideality of time," *Philosophy of Science* **83**(5), 1050–1058.

Marathe, K. (1972), "A condition for paracompactness of a manifold," *Journal of Differential Geometry* **7**(3–4), 571–573.

Martens, N. C. & Lehmkuhl, D. (2020), "Dark matter = modified gravity? Scrutinising the spacetime–matter distinction through the modified gravity/dark matter lens," *Studies in History and Philosophy of Modern Physics* **72**, 237–250.

Mashhoon, B. (2017), *Nonlocal Gravity*, Oxford University Press.

McKenzie, K. (2022), *Fundamentality and Grounding*, Cambridge University Press.

Melia, J. (1999), "Holes, haecceitism and two conceptions of determinism," *The British Journal for the Philosophy of Science* **50**(4), 639–664.

Menon, T., Linnemann, N., & Read, J. (2020), "Clocks and chronogeometry: Rotating spacetimes and the relativistic null hypothesis," *The British Journal for the Philosophy of Science* **71**, 1287–1317.

Minguzzi, E. (2019), "Lorentzian causality theory," *Living Reviews in Relativity* **22**(1), 1–202.

Misner, C. W., Thorne, K. S., & Wheeler, J. A. (1973), *Gravitation*, W. H. Freeman.

Myrvold, W. C. (2019), "How could relativity be anything other than physical?" *Studies in History and Philosophy of Modern Physics* **67**, 137–143.

Navarro, J. & Sancho, J. B. (2008), "On the naturalness of Einstein's equation," *Journal of Geometry and Physics* **58**(8), 1007–1014.

Nguyen, J. (2017), "Scientific representation and theoretical equivalence," *Philosophy of Science* **84**(5), 982–995.

Norton, J. (2020), "The hole argument against everything," *Foundations of Physics* **50**(4), 360–378.

Norton, J. D. (2008), "Why constructive relativity fails," *The British Journal for the Philosophy of Science* **59**(4), 821–834.

Norton, J. D. (2012), "Approximation and idealization: Why the difference matters," *Philosophy of Science* **79**(2), 207–232.

Norton, J. D., Pooley, O., & Read, J. (2023), "The hole argument," *in* E. N. Zalta & U. Nodelman, eds., *The Stanford Encyclopedia of Philosophy*, Summer 2023 ed., Metaphysics Research Lab, Stanford University.

O'Raifeartaigh, C., O'Keeffe, M., Nahm, W., & Mitton, S. (2018), "One hundred years of the cosmological constant: From 'superfluous stunt' to dark energy," *The European Physical Journal H* **43**(1), 73–117.

Petit, J. & d'Agostini, G. (2014), "Negative mass hypothesis in cosmology and the nature of dark energy," *Astrophysics and Space Science* **354**(2), 611–615.

Pfister, H. & King, M. (2015), *Inertia and Gravitation: The Fundamental Nature and Structure of Spacetime*, Springer.

Pitts, J. B. (2010), "Gauge-invariant localization of infinitely many gravitational energies from all possible auxiliary structures," *General Relativity and Gravitation* **42**(3), 601–622.

Pooley, O. (2013), "Substantivalist and relationalist approaches to spacetime," *in* R. Batterman, ed., *The Oxford Handbook of Philosophy of Physics*, Oxford University Press, pp. 522–586.

Pooley, O. (2021), "The hole argument," *in* E. Knox & A. Wilson, eds., *The Routledge Companion to Philosophy of Physics*, Routledge, pp. 145–159.

Ray, C. (1990), "The cosmological constant: Einstein's greatest mistake?" *Studies in History and Philosophy of Science* **21**(4), 589–604.

Read, J. (2020), "Functional gravitational energy," *The British Journal for the Philosophy of Science* **71**(1), 205–232.

Read, J. (2023), *Background Independence in Classical and Quantum Gravity*, Oxford University Press.

Read, J., Brown, H. R., & Lehmkuhl, D. (2018), "Two miracles of general relativity," *Studies in History and Philosophy of Modern Physics* **64**, 14–25.

Read, J. & Menon, T. (2021), "The limitations of inertial frame spacetime functionalism," *Synthese* **199**(S2), 229–251.

Rindler, W. (1960), *Special Relativity*, Oliver and Boyd.

Roberts, B. W. (2020), "Regarding 'Leibniz equivalence'," *Foundations of Physics* **50**(4), 250–269.

Rovelli, C. (1997), "Halfway through the woods: Contemporary research on space and time," *in* J. Earman & J. Norton, eds., *The Cosmos of Science*, University of Pittsburgh Press, pp. 180–223.

Rugh, S. E. & Zinkernagel, H. (2002), "The quantum vacuum and the cosmological constant problem," *Studies in History and Philosophy of Modern Physics* **33**(4), 663–705.

Rugh, S. E. & Zinkernagel, H. (2009), "On the physical basis of cosmic time," *Studies in History and Philosophy of Modern Physics* **40**(1), 1–19.

Rugh, S. E. & Zinkernagel, H. (2017), "Limits of time in cosmology," *in* K. Chamcham, J. Silk, J. Barrow, & S. Saunders, eds., *The Philosophy of Cosmology*, Cambridge University Press, pp. 377–395.

Ryckman, T. (2005), *The Reign of Relativity: Philosophy in Physics 1915–1925*, Oxford University Press.

Schneider, M. D. (2020), "What's the problem with the cosmological constant?" *Philosophy of Science* **87**(1), 1–20.

Sklar, L. (1977), "Facts, conventions, and assumptions in the theory of space time," *in* J. Earman, C. Glymour, & J. Stachel, eds., *Foundations of Space-Time Theories*, University of Minnesota Press, pp. 206–274.

Smeenk, C. (2013), "Philosophy of cosmology," *in* R. Batterman, ed., *The Oxford Handbook of Philosophy of Physics*, Oxford University Press, pp. 607–652.

Smeenk, C. & Wüthrich, C. (2011), "Time travel and time machines," *in* C. Callender, ed., *The Oxford Handbook of Philosophy of Time*, Oxford University Press, pp. 577–630.

Smeenk, C. & Wüthrich, C. (2021), "Determinism and general relativity," *Philosophy of Science* **88**(4), 638–664.

Smith, N. J. (2021), "Time Travel," *in* E. N. Zalta, ed., *The Stanford Encyclopedia of Philosophy*, Fall 2021 ed., Metaphysics Research Lab, Stanford University.

Steen, L. A. & Seebach, J. A. (1978), *Counterexamples in Topology*, 2nd ed., Springer.

Synge, J. L. (1960), *Relativity: The General Theory*, North-Holland.

Szabados, L. (1992), "On canonical pseudotensors, Sparling's form and Noether currents," *Classical and Quantum Gravity* **9**(11), 2521.

Szabados, L. B. (2009), "Quasi-local energy-momentum and angular momentum in general relativity," *Living Reviews in Relativity* **12**(1), 1–163.

Tahko, T. E. (2018), "Fundamentality," *in* E. N. Zalta, ed., *The Stanford Encyclopedia of Philosophy*, Fall 2018 ed., Metaphysics Research Lab, Stanford University.

Teitel, T. (2021), "What theoretical equivalence could not be," *Philosophical Studies* **178**(12), 4119–4149.

Vassallo, A. (2020), "Dependence relations in general relativity," *European Journal for Philosophy of Science* **10**(1), 1–28.

Visser, M. (2003), "The quantum physics of chronology protection," *in* G. Gibbons, E. P. S. Shellard, & S. J. Rankin, eds., *The Future of Theoretical Physics and Cosmology*, Cambridge University Press, pp. 161–176.

Wald, R. M. (1984), *General Relativity*, University of Chicago Press.

Weatherall, J. O. (2011), "On (some) explanations in physics," *Philosophy of Science* **78**(3), 421–447.

Weatherall, J. O. (2014), "Against dogma: On superluminal propagation in classical electromagnetism," *Studies in History and Philosophy of Modern Physics* **48**(2), 109–123.

Weatherall, J. O. (2017), "Inertial motion, explanation, and the foundations of classical spacetime theories," *in* D. Lehmkuhl, G. Schiemann, & E. Scholz, eds., *Towards a Theory of Spacetime Theories*, Birkhäuser, pp. 13–42.

Weatherall, J. O. (2018), "Regarding the 'hole argument'," *The British Journal for the Philosophy of Science* **69**(2), 329–350.

Weatherall, J. O. (2019), "Conservation, inertia, and spacetime geometry," *Studies in History and Philosophy of Modern Physics* **67**, 144–159.

Weatherall, J. O. (2020*a*), "Geometry and motion in general relativity," *in* C. Beisbart, T. Sauer, & C. Wüthrich, eds., *Thinking about Space and Time*, Springer, pp. 207–226.

Weatherall, J. O. (2020*b*), "Some philosophical prehistory of the (Earman-Norton) hole argument," *Studies in History and Philosophy of Modern Physics* **70**, 79–87.

Weaver, C. G. (2020), "On the argument from physics and general relativity," *Erkenntnis* **85**(2), 333–373.

Weinstein, S. (1996), "Strange couplings and space-time structure," *Philosophy of Science* **63**(S3), S63–S70.

Weinstein, S. (2006), "Superluminal signaling and relativity," *Synthese* **148**(2), 381–399.

Weisberg, J. & Taylor, J. (2005), "The relativistic binary pulsar b1913+16: Thirty years of observations and analysis," *in* F. Rasio & I. Stairs, eds., *Binary Radio Pulsars*, Vol. 328 of *Astronomical Society of the Pacific Conference Series*, pp. 25–32.

Wong, W. W.-Y. (2011), "Regular hyperbolicity, dominant energy condition and causality for Lagrangian theories of maps," *Classical and Quantum Gravity* **28**(21), 215008.

Acknowledgments

Writing this little Element was possible through a sabbatical from the University of Minnesota and stimulating visits at the Centre for Philosophy of Natural and Social Science at the London School of Economics, and the Universities of Oxford (St Catherine's and Corpus Christi Colleges), Bristol, and Bonn, the latter two as, respectively, a Next Generation Visiting Researcher and a Humboldt Fellow. For their helpful written comments on various sections, I thank Jeremy Butterfield, Juliusz Doboszewski, Jamee Elder, Henrique Gomes, Klaas Landsman, Dennis Lehmkuhl, Brian Pitts, Bryan Roberts, and two referees. I'm also grateful for feedback on various portions of this work presented at the Inter-University Centre Dubrovnik, the Universities of Birmingham, Bonn, Bristol, Geneva, Lisbon, Minnesota, Utrecht, Oslo, Oxford, and Wuppertal, as well as the London School of Economics and the Warsaw University of Technology. Finally, Jim Weatherall has my gratitude for his patience and encouragement through the whole process.

The Philosophy of Physics

James Owen Weatherall
University of California, Irvine

James Owen Weatherall is Professor of Logic and Philosophy of Science at the University of California, Irvine. He is the author, with Cailin O'Connor, of *The Misinformation Age: How False Beliefs Spread* (Yale, 2019), which was selected as a *New York Times* Editors' Choice and Recommended Reading by *Scientific American*. His previous books were *Void: The Strange Physics of Nothing* (Yale, 2016) and the *New York Times* bestseller *The Physics of Wall Street: A Brief History of Predicting the Unpredictable* (Houghton Mifflin Harcourt, 2013). He has published approximately fifty peer-reviewed research articles in journals in leading physics and philosophy of science journals and has delivered over 100 invited academic talks and public lectures.

About the Series

This Cambridge Elements series provides concise and structured introductions to all the central topics in the philosophy of physics. The Elements in the series are written by distinguished senior scholars and bright junior scholars with relevant expertise, producing balanced, comprehensive coverage of multiple perspectives in the philosophy of physics.